FIAT 126 Owners Workshop Manual

by J H Haynes
Member of the Guild of Motoring Writers

and P G Strasman
ISTC

Models covered:

Covers the Standard, L and Sunroof models
fitted with the 594 cc engine

Does not fully cover the DeVille model

ISBN 0 85696 305 4

1546/305

© Haynes Publishing Group 1977

Printed in England

Haynes Publishing Group
Sparkford Yeovil Somerset England
distributed in the USA by
Haynes Publications Inc
9421 Winnetka Avenue
Chatsworth
California 91311 USA

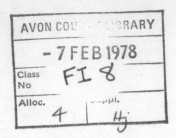
Acknowledgements

Our thanks to Fiat (England) Limited who kindly supplied the technical information and certain of the illustrations reproduced in this manual. Woolf, Laing, Christie and Partners were also very helpful. Castrol Limited supplied lubrication data, and the Champion Sparking Plug Company supplied the illustrations showing the various spark plug conditions. The bodywork repair photographs used in this manual were provided by Lloyds Industries Limited who supply 'Turtle-Wax', 'Dupli-color Holts', and other Holts range products.

We are particularly grateful to Mr. F. Martindale who kindly loaned us his car as project vehicle.

Lastly, thanks are due to all of those people at Sparkford who helped in the production of this manual. Particularly, Brian Horsfall and Leon Martindale (member of the Master Photographers Association) who carried out the mechanical work and took the photographs respectively; Ted Frenchum who planned the layout of each page and Rod Grainger the editor.

About this manual

Its aim

The aim of this book is to help you get the best value from your car. It can do so in two ways. First it can help you decide what work must be done, even should you choose to get it done by a garage, the routine maintenance and the diagnosis and course of action when random faults occur. It is hoped that you will also use the second and fuller purpose by tackling the work yourself. This can give you the satisfaction of doing the job yourself. On the simpler jobs it may even be quicker than booking the car into a garage and going there twice, to leave and collect it. Perhaps most important, much money can be saved by avoiding the costs a garage must charge to cover their labour and overheads.

Haynes Owner's Workshop Manuals are the *only* manuals, available to the public, which are actually written from practical experience. We buy an example of the vehicle to be covered by the manual. Then, in our own workshops, the major components of that vehicle are stripped and rebuilt by the author and a mechanic: at the same time all sequences are photographed. By doing this work ourselves, we encounter the same problems as you will and having overcome these problems, we can provide you with practical solutions.

The book has drawings and descriptions to show the function of the various components so that their layout can be understood. Then the tasks are described and photographed in a step by step sequence so that even a novice can cope with complicated work. Such a person is the very one to buy a car needing repair yet unable to afford garage costs.

The jobs are described assuming only normal tools are available, and not special tools, but a reasonable outfit of tools will be a worthwhile investment. Many special workshop tools produced by the makers merely speed the work, and in these cases guidance is given as to how to do the job without them. On a very few occasions the special tool

is essential to prevent damage to components, then its use is described. Though it might be possible to borrow the tool, such work may have to be entrusted to the official agent.

To avoid labour costs a garage will often give a cheaper repair by fitting a reconditioned assembly. The home mechanic can be helped by this book to diagnose the fault and make a repair using only a minor spare part. The classic case is repairing a non-charging dynamo by fitting new brushes.

Using the manual

The manual is divided into eleven Chapters - each covering a logical sub-division of the vehicle. The individual Chapters are divided into Sections, and the Sections into numbered paragraphs.

Procedures, once described in the text, are not normally repeated. If it is necessary to refer to another Chapter the reference will be given in Chapter number and Section number.

There are two types of illustration: (1) Figures which are numbered according to Chapter and sequence of occurrence in that Chapter. (2) Photographs which have a reference number on their caption. All photographs apply to the Chapter in which they occur so that the reference figure pinpoints the pertinent Section and paragraph number.

When the left or right side of the car is mentioned it is as if looking forward from the rear of the car.

Great effort has been made to ensure that this book is complete and up to-date. However, the vehicle manufacturers continually modify their cars, even in retrospect, without giving notice.

Whilst every care is taken to ensure that the information in this manual is correct no liability can be accepted by the authors or publishers for loss, damage or injury caused by any errors in, or omissions from, the information given.

Introduction to the Fiat 126

The Fiat 126 was introduced in July 1973 to be the eventual successor to the Fiat 500 which it has now become.

Major improvements in comparison with the 500 include an all synchromesh gearbox and more modern styling.

The car provides extremely low-cost transportation and in consequence its power and comfort cannot be expected to match larger and more expensive vehicles.

It is strong and reliable and very simply serviced and is adequate from the points of view of equipment and accessories in what is essentially an 'about town' car.

The Fiat 126 is produced in a single two-door body style but a variation having a sunroof and opening rear side windows can be specified.

Contents

Note: *Specifications, torque wrench settings and general descriptions are given in each Chapter immediately after the 'list of contents'. Where applicable, fault diagnosis is given at the end of each appropriate Chapter.*

FIAT 126 (1976 model)

Buying spare parts and vehicle identification numbers

Buying spare parts

Spare parts are available from many sources, for example Fiat garages, other garages and accessory shops, and motor factors. Our advice regarding spare part sources is as follows:

Officially appointed Fiat garages - This is the best source of parts which are peculiar to your car and are otherwise not generally available (eg; complete cylinder heads, internal gearbox components, badges, interior trim etc). It is also the only place at which you should buy parts if your car is still under warranty: non-Fiat components may invalidate the warranty. To be sure of obtaining the correct parts it will always be necessary to give the storeman your car's engine and chassis number, and if possible, to take the old part along for positive identification. Remember that many parts are available on a factory exchange scheme - any parts returned should always be clean! It obviously makes good sense to go straight to the specialists on your car for this type of part for they are best equipped to supply you.

Other garages and accessory shops - These are often very good places to buy materials and components needed for the maintenance of your car (eg spark plugs, bulbs, fanbelts, oils and greases, touch-up paint, filler paste, etc). They also sell general accessories, usually have convenient opening hours, charge lower prices and can often be found not far from home.

Motor factors - Good factors will stock all of the more important components which wear out relatively quickly (eg: cylinders/pipes/hoses/seals/shoes and pads etc). Motor factors will often provide new or reconditioned components on a part exchange basis - this can save a considerable amount of money.

Vehicle identification numbers

The data plate is located within the luggage boot and contains details of chassis type and number, engine type and number for spares and the body paintwork reference number (photo).

The engine type and number are stamped on the engine casting adjacent to the fuel pump mounting flange (photo).

The chassis type and number are located on the wing valance within the luggage boot (photo).

Data plate

Location of engine number

Location of chassis type and number

Tools and working facilities

Introduction

A selection of good tools is a fundamental requirement for anyone contemplating the maintenance and repair of a motor vehicle. For the owner who does not possess any, their purchase will prove a considerable expense, offsetting some of the savings made by doing-it-yourself. However, provided that the tools purchased are of good quality, they will last for many years and prove an extremely worthwhile investment.

To help the average owner to decide which tools are needed to carry out the various tasks detailed in this manual, we have compiled three lists of tools under the following headings: Maintenance and minor repair, Repair and overhaul, and Special. The newcomer to practical mechanics should start off with the 'Maintenance and minor repair' tool kit and confine himself to the simpler jobs around the vehicle. Then, as his confidence and experience grows, he can undertake more difficult tasks, buying extra tools as, and when, they are needed. In this way, a 'Maintenance and minor repair' tool kit can be built-up into a 'Repair and overhaul' tool kit over a considerable period of time without any major cash outlays. The experienced do-it-yourself will have a tool kit good enough for most repair and overhaul procedures and will add tools from the 'Special' category when he feels the expense is justified by the amount of use these tools will be put to.

It is obviously not possible to cover the subject of tools fully here. For those who wish to learn more about tools and their use there is a book entitled 'How to Choose and Use Car Tools' available from the publishers of this manual.

Maintenance and minor repair tool kit

The tools given in this list should be considered as a minimum requirement if routine maintenance, servicing and minor repair operations are to be undertaken. We recommend the purchase of combination spanners (ring one end, open-ended the other); although more expensive than open-ended ones, they do give the advantages of both types of spanner.

> Combination spanners - 10, 11, 13, 14, 17 mm
> Adjustable spanner - 9 inch
> Engine sump/gearbox/rear axle drain plug key (where applicable)
> Spark plug gap adjustment tool
> Spark plug spanner (with rubber insert)
> Set of feeler gauges
> Brake adjuster spanner (where applicable)
> Brake bleed nipple spanner
> Screwdriver - 4 in. long x ¼ in. dia. (plain)
> Screwdriver - 4 in. long x ¼ in. dia. (crosshead)
> Combination pliers - 6 inch
> Hacksaw, junior
> Tyre pump
> Tyre pressure gauge
> Grease gun (where applicable)
> Oil can
> Fine emery cloth (1 sheet)
> Wire brush (small)
> Funnel (medium size)

Repair and overhaul tool kit

These tools are virtually essential for anyone undertaking any major repairs to a motor vehicle, and are additional to those given in the Basic list. Included in this list is a comprehensive set of sockets. Although these are expensive they will be found invaluable as they are so versatile - particularly if various drives are included in the set. We recommend the ½ inch square drive type, as this can be used with most proprietary torque wrenches. If you cannot afford a socket set, even bought piecemeal, then inexpensive tubular box spanners are a useful alternative.

The tools in this list will occasionally need to be supplemented by tools from the Special list.

> Sockets (or box spanners) to cover range 6 to 27 mm
> Reversible ratchet drive (for use with sockets)
> Extension piece, 10 inch (for use with sockets)
> Universal joint (for use with sockets)
> Torque wrench (for use with sockets)
> 'Mole' wrench - 8 inch
> Ball pein hammer
> Soft-faced hammer, plastic or rubber
> Screwdriver - 6 in. long x 5/16 in. dia. (plain)
> Screwdriver - 2 in. long x 5/16 in. square (plain)
> Screwdriver - 1½ in. long x ¼ in. dia. (crosshead)
> Screwdriver - 3 in. long x 1/8 in. dia. (electricians)
> Pliers - electricians side cutters
> Pliers - needle nosed
> Pliers - circlip (internal and external)
> Cold chisel - ½ inch
> Scriber (this can be made by grinding the end of a broken hacksaw blade)
> Scraper (this can be made by flattening and sharpening one end of a piece of copper pipe)
> Centre punch
> Pin punch
> Hacksaw
> Valve grinding tool
> Steel rule/straight edge
> Allen keys
> Selection of files
> Wire brush (large)
> Axle stands
> Jack (strong scissor or hydraulic type)

Special tools

The tools in this list are those which are not used regularly, are expensive to buy, or which need to be used in accordance with their manufacturers instructions. Unless relatively difficult mechanical jobs are undertaken frequently, it will not be economic to buy many of these tools. Where this is the case, you could consider clubbing together with friends (or a motorists club) to make a joint purchase, or borrowing the tools against a deposit from a local garage or tool hire specialist.

The following list contains only those tools and instruments freely available to the public, and not those special tools produced by the vehicle manufacturers specifically for its dealer network. You will find occasional references to these manufacturers special tools in the text of this manual. Generally, an alternative method of doing the job without the vehicle manufacturers special tool is given. However, sometimes there is no alternative to using them. Where this is the case and the relevant tool cannot be bought or borrowed you will have to entrust the work to a franchised garage.

Valve spring compressor
Piston ring compressor
Ball joint separator
Universal hub/bearing puller
Impact screwdriver
Micrometer and/or vernier gauge
Carburettor flow balancing device (where applicable)
Dial gauge
Stroboscopic timing light
Dwell angle meter/tachometer
Universal electrical multi-meter
Cylinder compression gauge
Lifting tackle
Trolley jack
Light with extension lead

Buying tools

For practically all tools, a tool factor is the best source since he will have a very comprehensive range compared with the average garage or accessory shop. Having said that, accessory shops often offer excellent quality tools at discount prices, so it pays to shop around.

Remember, you do not have to buy the most expensive items on the shelf, but it is always advisable to steer clear of the very cheap tools. There are plenty of good tools around, at reasonable prices, so ask the proprietor or manager of the shop for advice before making a purchase.

Care and maintenance of tools

Having purchased a reasonable tool kit, it is necessary to keep the tools in a clean and serviceable condition. After use, always wipe off any dirt, grease and metal particles using a clean, dry cloth, before putting the tools away. Never leave them lying around after they have been used. A simple tool rack on the garage or workshop wall, for items such as screwdrivers and pliers is a good idea. Store all normal spanners and sockets in a metal box. Any measuring instruments, gauges, meters, etc., must be carefully stored where they cannot be damaged or become rusty.

Take a little care when the tools are used. Hammer heads inevitably become marked and screwdrivers lose the keen edge on their blades from time-to-time. A little timely attention with emery cloth or a file will soon restore items like this to a good serviceable finish.

Working facilities

Not to be forgotten when discussing tools, is the workshop itself. If anything more than routine maintenance is to be carried out, some form of suitable working area becomes essential.

It is appreciated that many an owner mechanic is forced by circumstances to remove an engine or similar item, without the benefit of a garage or workshop. Having done this, any repairs should always be done under the cover of a roof.

Wherever possible, any dismantling should be done on a clean flat workbench or table at a suitable working height.

Any workbench needs a vice: one with a jaw opening 4 in. (100 mm) is suitable for most jobs. As mentioned previously, some clean dry storage space is also required for tools, as well as the lubricants, cleaning fluids, touch-up paints and so on which soon become necessary.

Another item which may be required, and which has a much more general usage, is an electric drill with a chuck capacity of at least 5/16 in. (8 mm). This, together with a good range of twist drills, is virtually essential for fitting accessories such as wing mirrors and reversing lights.

Last, but not least, always keep a supply of old newspapers and clean lint-free rags available, and try to keep any working area as clean as possible.

Spanner jaw gap comparison table

Jaw gap (in)	Spanner size
0.250	1/4 in. AF
0.275	7 mm AF
0.312	5/16 in. AF
0.315	8 mm AF
0.340	11/32 in. AF/1/8 in. Whitworth
0.354	9 mm AF
0.375	3/8 in. AF
0.393	10 mm AF
0.433	11 mm AF
0.437	7/16 in. AF
0.445	3/16 in. Whitworth 1/4in. BSF
0.472	12 mm AF
0.500	1/2 in. AF
0.512	13 mm AF
0.525	1/4 in. Whitworth/5/16 in. BSF
0.551	14 mm AF
0.562	9/16 in. AF
0.590	15 mm AF
0.600	5/16 in. Whitworth/3/8 in. BSF
0.625	5/8 in. AF
0.629	16 mm AF
0.669	17 mm AF
0.687	11/16 in. AF
0.708	18 mm AF
0.710	3/8 in. Whitworth/7/16 in. BSF
0.748	19 mm AF
0.750	3/4 in AF
0.812	13/16 in AF
0.820	7/16 in. Whitworth/1/2 in. BSF
0.866	22 mm AF
0.875	7/8 in. AF
0.920	1/2 in Whitworth/9/16 in. BSF
0.937	15/16 in. AF
0.944	24 mm AF
1.000	1 in. AF
1.010	9/16 in. Whitworth/5/8 in. BSF
1.023	26 mm AF
1.062	1 1/16 in. AF/27 mm AF
1.100	5/8 in. Whitworth /11/16 in. BSF
1.125	1 1/8 in AF
1.181	30 mm AF
1.200	11/16 in. Whitworth/3/4 in. BSF
1.250	1 1/4 in. AF
1.259	32 mm AF
1.300	3/4 in. Whitworth/7/8 in. BSF
1.312	1 5/16 in. AF
1.390	13/16 in. Whitworth/15/16 in. BSF
1.417	36 mm AF
1.437	1 7/16 in. AF
1.480	7/8 in. Whitworth/1 in. BSF
1.500	1 1/2 in. AF
1.574	40 mm AF/15/16 in. Whitworth
1.614	41 mm AF
1.625	1 5/8 in. AF
1.670	1 in. Whitworth/1 1/8 in. BSF
1.687	1 11/16 in. AF
1.811	46 mm AF
1.812	1 13/16 in. AF
1.860	1 1/8 in. Whitworth/1 1/4 in. BSF
1.875	1 7/8 in. AF
1.968	50 mm AF
2.000	2 in. AF
2.050	1 1/4 in. Whitworth/1 3/8 in. BSF
2.165	55 mm AF
2.362	60 mm AF

Routine maintenance

Maintenance is essential for ensuring safety and desirable for the purpose of getting the best in terms of performance and economy from the car. Over the years the need for periodic lubrication - oiling, greasing, and so on - has been drastically reduced if not totally eliminated. This has unfortunately tended to lead some owners to think that because no such action is required the items either no longer exist or will last for ever. This is a serious delusion. It follows therefore that the largest initial element of maintenance is visual examination. This may lead to repairs or renewal.

Every 250 miles (400 km) or weekly

Steering
Check the tyre pressures including the spare wheel.
Examine tyres for wear or damage.

Brakes
Check brake fluid reservoir level.
Try an emergency stop. Are automatic adjusters effective or has pedal travel increased?

Electrical
Check all lamp bulbs.
Check battery electrolyte level.
Check operation of wipers and horn.
Top-up windscreen washer reservoir.

Engine
Check oil level and top-up if necessary (photo).

Topping up with engine oil

Every 6,000 miles (9,600 km)

Steering
Check steering box oil level and top-up.
Apply grease gun to front suspension (king pin) nipples.
Check steering linkage balljoints for wear.
Check front wheel alignment.

Brakes
Check for lining wear.
Adjust handbrake cables.

Electrical
Check dynamo/fanbelt tension.
Check headlamp alignment.

Engine
Check valve clearances.
Renew air cleaner element.
Check carburettor adjustment.
Renew spark plugs.
Check distributor contact point gap.
Check ignition timing.
Clean carburettor fuel filter gauze.
Clean fuel pump filter.

Body
Lubricate hinges and locks.

Clutch
Check clutch free-movement and adjust if necessary.

Every 18,000 miles (28,000 km)

Steering
Check, repack and adjust front wheel bearings.

Transmission
Check condition of driveshaft flexible boots.
Drain and refill unit with specified oil.

General
Check all nuts and bolts to specified torque wrench settings.

Every 36,000 miles (58,000 km)

Brakes
Drain hydraulic system, renew all cylinder seals and refill with fresh fluid.

Exhaust system
Check for corrosion and renew if necessary.

Underbody
Clean and take rust preventative measures.

General dimensions, weights and capacities

Dimensions and weights

Overall length	...	...	...	...	...	...	...	...	...	120.2 in (305. 4 cm)
Overall width	...	...	...	...	...	...	...	...	...	53.8 in (137.7 cm)
Overall height	...	...	...	...	...	...	...	...	...	52.4 in (133.5 cm)
Wheelbase	...	...	...	...	...	...	...	...	...	72.4 in (184. 0 cm)
Front track	...	...	...	...	...	...	...	...	...	44.9 in (114. 2 cm)
Rear track	...	...	...	...	...	...	...	...	...	47.3 in (120.3 cm)
Kerb weight	...	...	...	...	...	...	...	...	...	1279 lb (580 kg)

Capacities

Fuel tank	...	...	...	...	...	...	...	...	...	4.6 Imp. gallons (20.5 litres)
Engine oil	...	...	...	...	...	...	...	...	...	4.5 Imp. pints (2.6 litres)
Transmission	...	...	...	...	...	...	...	...	...	2 Imp. pints (1.13 litres)
Steering box	...	...	...	...	...	...	...	...	...	4.25 fl. oz. (120.3 ml)
Windscreen washer reservoir	...	...	...	...	...	...	...	...	3.5 Imp. pints (1.99 litres)

Jacking and towing

The jack supplied with the car should only be used for changing a roadwheel. When carrying out repairs or maintenance work, use a hydraulic or screw jack under the jacking points and supplement these with axle stands or blocks.

To jack up the front or rear of the car, place the jack under the front or rear crossmember. When jacking under the rear crossmember use a wooden block as an insulator.

If your car is being towed, thread the tow rope through the two holes in the small bracket located under the crossmember. If you are towing another small vehicle, attach the tow rope to the jacking bracket at the base of the crossmember (photo).

Front tow rope attachment plate

Rear tow rope attachment plate

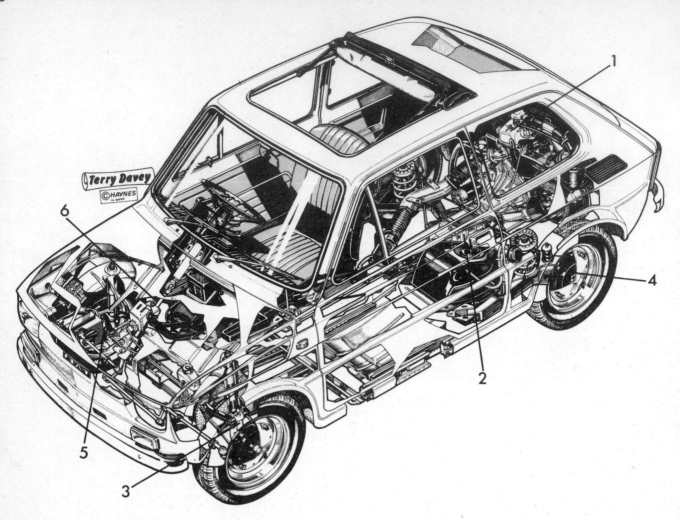

Terry Davey
©HAYNES

Recommended lubricants and fluids

Components	Lubricant
1 Engine	Castrol GTX
2 Transmission	Castrol Hypoy
3 Front wheel bearings	Castrol LM Grease
4 Rear wheel bearings	Castrol LM Grease
5 King pins	Castrol LM Grease
6 Steering gear	Castrol Hypoy B
7 Brake master cylinder reservoir	Castrol Girling Universal Brake and Clutch Fluid

Additionally Castrol Everyman oil can be used to lubricate door, boot and bonnet hinges, and locks, pivots etc.

Note: The above recommendations are general: lubrication requirements vary from territory-to-territory. Consult the operators handbook supplied with your car.

Chapter 1 Engine

Contents

Specifications

Engine (general)

Engine type ...	Two cylinder, vertical in-line, air-cooled, overhead valve, rear mounted.
Bore ...	2.894 in (73.5 mm)
Stroke ...	2.756 in (70.0 mm)
Displacement ...	36.23cu in (594 cc)
Compression ratio ...	7.5 : 1
Maximum HP (DIN rating) @ 4800 rev/min ...	23
Maximum torque @ 3400 rev/min ...	29 lb/ft (4 kg/m)

Crankcase and cylinder barrels

Cylinder bore diameter:
Grading:

A ...	2.8937 to 2.8941 in (73.500 to 73.510 mm)
B ...	2.8941 to 2.8945 in (73.510 to 73.520 mm)
C ...	2.8945 to 2.8949 in (73.520 to 73.530 mm)

Camshaft bore in crankcase:

Timing gear end ...	1.6937 to 1.6946 in (43.020 to 43.045 mm)
Flywheel end ...	0.8667 to 0.8675 in (22.015 to 22.036 mm)
Camshaft bearing running clearance ...	0.0006 to 0.0025 in (0.015 to 0.055 mm)
Cam followers bore in crankcase ...	0.8662 to 0.8669 in (22.003 to 22.021 mm)
Cam followers clearance in crankcase ...	0.0003 to 0.0017 in (0.007 to 0.043 mm)
Connecting rod big-end bore (diameter) ...	1.8555 to 1.8560 in (47.130 to 47.142 mm)
Big-end bearing thickness (standard size) ...	0.0604 to 0.0607 in (1.534 to 1.543 mm)
Big-end bearing undersizes ...	0.01 - 0.02 - 0.03 - 0.04 in (0.254 - 0.508 - 0.762 - 1.016 mm)
Connecting rod small end bush (diameter) in connecting rod ...	0.8637 to 0.8650 in (21.939 to 21.972 mm)
Small end bush internal diameter (reamed) ...	0.7874 to 0.7876 in (20.000 to 20.006 mm)
Small end bush undersizes ...	0.0076 - 0.0196 in (0.2 - 0.5 mm)
Gudgeon pin clearance in small end bush ...	0.0002 to 0.0006 in (0.005 to 0.016 mm)

Specifications - continued

Connecting rod running clearance on crankpins:

Up to 1974	0.0004 to 0,0024 in (0.011 to 0.061 mm)
November 1974 on	0.0009 to 0,0029 in (0.024 to 0.074 mm)

Pistons

Piston diameter (at right angles to gudgeon pin);
Grading:

A (up to 1974)	2.8905 to 2.8909 in (73.420 to 73.430 mm)
A (1974 on)	2.8901 to 2.8905 in (73.410 to 73.420 mm)
B (up to 1974)	2.8909 to 2.8913 in (73.430 to 73.440 mm)
B (1974 on)	2.8905 to 2.8909 in (73.420 to 73.430 mm)
C (up to 1974)	2.8913 to 2.8917 in (73.440 to 73.450 mm)
C (1974 on)	2.8909 to 2.8913 in (73.430 to 73.440 mm)
Piston oversizes	0.0079 - 0.0157 - 0.0236 in (0.2 - 0.4 - 0.6 mm)
Gudgeon pin bore (diameter) in piston	0.7872 to 0.7874 in (19.995 to 20.000 mm)

Piston ring groove width:

Top	0.0604 to 0.0612 in (1.535 to 1.555 mm)
Centre	0.0800 to 0.0807 in (2.030 to 2.050 mm)
Bottom	0.1562 to 0.1569 in (3.967 to 3.987 mm)
Gudgeon pin diameter	0.7870 to 0.7872 in (19.990 to 19.995 mm)
Gudgeon pin oversize	0.0079 in (0.2 mm)

Piston ring thickness:

Top compression	0.0582 to 0.0587 in (1.478 to 1.490 mm)
Centre oil control	0.0778 to 0.0783 in (1.978 to 1.990 mm)
Bottom oil control	0.1544 to 0.1549 in (3.925 to 3.937 mm)
Piston ring oversizes	0.0079 - 0.0157 - 0.0236 in (0.2 - 0.4 - 0.6 mm)

Piston clearance in cylinder barrel (measured at right angles to
gudgeon pin and 2¼ in down from crown) (57.15 mm):

Up to 1974	0.0028 to 0.0035 in (0.070 to 0.090 mm)
1974 on	0.0031 to 0.0039 in (0.080 to 0.100 mm)

Piston ring end-gap:

Top	0.0098 to 0.0157 in (0.25 to 0.40 mm)
Centre at bottom	0.0080 to 0.0136 in (0.20 to 0.35 mm)
Maximum weight differential between pistons	0.902 (0.5 g)

Valves

Valve guide bore (diameter) in cylinder head	0.5492 to 0.5503 in (13.950 to 13.977 mm)

Valve guide outside diameter:

Standard	0.5527 to 0.5534 in (14.040 to 14.058 mm)
Oversize	0.5535 to 0.5543 in (14.060 to 14.078 mm)
Valve guide internal diameter	0.3158 to 0.3165 in (8.022 to 8.040 mm)
Valve stem diameter	0.3139 to 0.3146 in (7.974 to 7.992 mm)
Valve stem clearance in guide	0.0012 to 0.0026 in (0.030 to 0.066 mm)
Valve seat angle	45° ± 5′
Valve face angle	45° 30′ ± 5′

Valve head diameter:

Inlet	1.26 in (32.0 mm)
Exhaust	1.16 in (28.0 mm)

Valve clearances (COLD):

Inlet	0.0078 in (0.20 mm)
Exhaust	0.0098 in (0.25 mm)

Valve spring free length:

Inner spring	1.5748 in (40.0 mm)
Outer spring	1.9685 in (50.0 mm)

Valve timing:
Inlet opens:

Up to 1974	26° BTDC
1974 on	26° BTDC

Inlet closes:

Up to 1974	56° ABDC
1974 on	57° ABDC

Exhaust opens:

Up to 1974	66° BBDC
1974 on	66° BBDC

Exhaust closes:

Up to 1974	16° ATDC
1974 on	17° ATDC

Crankshaft

Main bearing journal diameter	2.1248 to 2.1256 in (53.970 to 53.990 mm)
Main bearing shell internal diameter	2.1274 to 2.1279 in (54.035 to 54.050 mm)
Main bearing undersizes	0.0079 - 0.0157 - 0.236 - 0.394 in (0.2 - 0.4 - 0.6 - 0.9 mm)
Main bearing running clearance	0.0081 to 0.0031 in (0.205 to 0.080 mm)
Crankpin diameter	1.7328 to 1.7336 in (44.013 to 44.033 mm)

Specifications - continued

Lubrication system

Clearance between oil pump gears and pump housing	0.0027 and 0.0051 in (0.070 and 0.130 mm)	
Oil pump gear endfloat	0.0012 to 0.0034 in (0.030 to 0.087 mm)	
Oil pressure (HOT)	35 to 43 lb/sq in (2.5 to 3 kg/sq cm)	
Oil capacity	4.4 Imp pints (2.5 litres/5.3 US pints)	

Torque wrench settings

	lb f ft	Nm
Cylinder head nuts	29	40
Connecting rod big-end nut	25	35
Flywheel bolt	25	35
Camshaft sprocket bolt	7	10
Rocker pedestal nut	18	25
Main bearing retainer bolts	22	30
Rear crossmember to body bolts	29	40
Rear mounting bracket to engine	36	50
Rear mounting insulator to crossmember	11	15
Spark plugs	22	30
Filter/pulley hollow bolt to crankshaft	108	149

1 General description

1 The engine is rear mounted and is of twin cylinder air-cooled type.
2 The vertical in-line cylinders are of cast-iron construction while the cylinder head and the crankcase are of light-alloy.
3 The crankshaft is supported in two main bearings.
4 Light-alloy pistons are used having an upper chromium plated compression ring and two lower oil control rings.
5 The overhead valve gear comprises valves, rockers, pushrods and tappets operated from the camshaft which is located in the crankcase.
6 Lubrication is by means of a gear type oil pump driven by a dog clutch at the forward end of the camshaft.
7 Cooling is by fan-generated forced draught. Cooling fins are cast into the cylinder block and the system incorporates ducting and a thermostat to control the volume of cooling air being exhausted depending upon the engine temperature level.
8 The engine/transmission unit which comprises the engine, the clutch, the gearbox and the final drive are mounted as one assembly

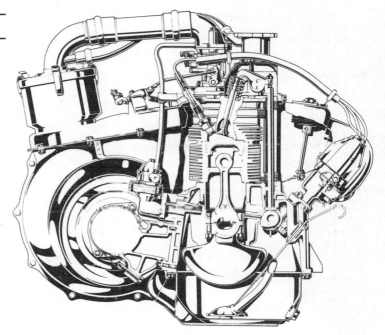

Fig. 1.2. Cut away view of engine (transverse)

on two flexible front mountings and one flexible/coil spring rear mounting.

2 Operations possible with engine in car

The following operations are possible without having to remove the engine from the car.
1 Removal and installation of the cylinder head.
2 Decarbonising and attention to valves.
3 Removal and installation of timing gear components.
4 Removal and installation of oil pump and centrifugal oil filter.
5 Removal and installation of the sump.
6 Removal and installation of the big-end bearings.
7 Removal and installation of the connecting rod/piston assemblies.
8 Removal and installation of the cylinder barrels.
If more overhead room to work is required for the last two operations, the rear crossmember can be unbolted and the engine lowered slightly on a jack.

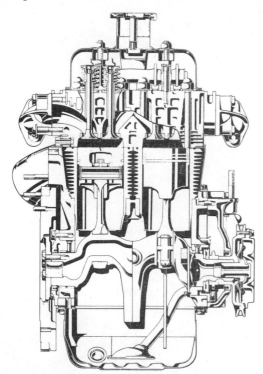

Fig. 1.1. Cut away view of engine (longitudinal)

3 Operations only possible with engine removed

The following work can only be carried out after removal of the engine from the car.

  1 *Removal and installation of the camshaft.*
  2 *Removal and installation of the crankshaft.*
  3 *Removal and installation of the main bearings.*
  4 *Renewal of the crankshaft front oil seal.*

Removal and installation of the flywheel can be carried out either by removing the engine or alternatively by withdrawing the gearbox and then unbolting the clutch mechanism.

4 Engine - method of removal

1   It is not very often that the engine and gearbox require major overhaul at one and the same time. It is therefore recommended that the engine is withdrawn separately from the rear of the car leaving the gearbox in position.
2   The gearbox can be removed independently towards the front of the car leaving the engine in position.
3   The engine combined with the transmission unit can be removed rearwards, as one unit if required, but all the engine and gearbox controls and the driveshaft must be disconnected, which is wasting time and effort if only one assembly is to be worked upon.

5 Engine - removal

1   Disconnect the battery which is located in the (front) boot.
2   Raise the rear of the car and support it securely on axle stands placed under the body side brackets.
3   Disconnect the engine compartment lid check strap (prise up the tab to release the anchor from the securing clip) and then withdraw the lid by sliding it out of its hinges after the single self-locking nut has been unscrewed (photo).
4   Disconnect the leads from the generator.
5   Disconnect the LT and HT leads from the ignition coil.
6   Disconnect the lead from the oil pressure switch (photo).
7   Disconnect the accelerator and choke controls from the carburettor.
8   Disconnect the fuel inlet pipe from the fuel pump. On some later models, disconnect the fuel return hose from the carburettor.
9   Disconnect the trunking which supplies cooling air to the engine fan unit.
10   Unbolt and remove the shield from above the exhaust silencer.
11   Disconnect the rear licence plate lamp leads at the connector plug (photo).
12   Working under the car, remove the under tray (photo).
13   Unbolt and remove the lower cover from the clutch bellhousing.
14   Unscrew and remove the lower bolts which secure the clutch bellhousing to the engine.
15   Extract the split pin and disconnect the operating cable from the starter motor switch.
16   Disconnect the two leads from the starter motor terminals.
17   Remove the bolts from the starter motor mounting flange which also secure the clutch bellhousing to the engine.
18   Disconnect the car interior heater ducting from the hot air outlet, by extracting the ratchet type plastic hose band.
19   Drain the engine oil.
20   Again working within the engine compartment, reach over the engine and unscrew and remove the upper bolts which secure the clutch bellhousing to the engine.
21   Take the weight of the engine on a trolley jack with a stout piece of timber placed under the unit in a crosswise attitude so that it supports the exhaust silencer on one side and the base of the cooling fan housing on the other. This arrangement will help to steady the engine and prevent it dropping on one side as it is withdrawn (photo).
22   Disconnect the coil spring type engine rear mounting by extracting the centre bolt (photo).
23   Unscrew and remove the two nuts at each end of the rear crossmember - note the earth strap which is located under one of the nuts (photo).

24   Remove the rear crossmember.
25   Withdraw the engine from the rear of the car (Fig. 1.4), supporting the gearbox on a second jack (photo).

6 Engine ancillaries - removal

With the engine removed from the car, the engine ancillary components can be detached at this stage by reference to the appropriate Chapters listed. Alternatively if complete dismantling of the engine is to be carried out, continue as described in Section 8 onwards.

  1 *Distributor complete with HT leads (Chapter 4).*
  2 *Exhaust silencer/manifold assembly (Chapter 3).*
  3 *Air cleaner and carburettor (Chapter 3).*
  4 *Fuel pump (Chapter 3).*
  5 *Generator (Chapter 10) (photo).*
  6 *The engine cooling fan assembly (Chapter 2).*
  7 *The engine air temperature regulating unit (Chapter 2).*
  8 *The clutch mechanism (Chapter 5).*

Fig. 1.3. Engine compartment (note lid check strap)

Fig. 1.4. Preparing to remove the engine on a trolley jack

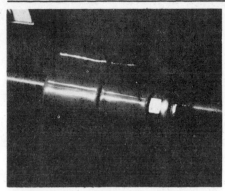

5.3 Self-locking nut on engine compartment lid hinge

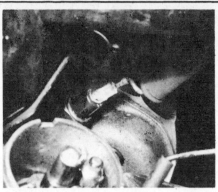

5.6 Location of oil pressure switch

5.11 Rear licence plate lead connector plug

5.12 Engine undertray

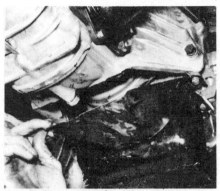

5.13 Removing lower cover from clutch bellhousing

15.21 Engine supported on trolley jack ready for removal

5.22 Engine rear mounting

5.23 Earth strap connection to rear crossmember bolt

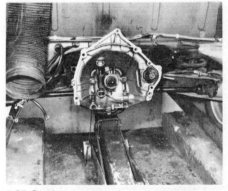

5.25 Gearbox supported on second jack

6.5 Engine withdrawn showing exhaust, dynamo and right-hand cooling casing and rocker cover removed

7 Engine - dismantling general

1 It is best to mount the engine on a dismantling stand but if one is not available, then stand the engine on a strong bench so as to be at a comfortable working height. Failing this, the engine will have to be stripped down on the floor.

2 During the dismantling process the greatest care should be taken to keep the exposed parts free from dirt. As an aid to achieving this, it is a sound scheme to thoroughly clean down the outside of the engine, removing all traces of oil and congealed dirt.

3 Use paraffin or a good water soluble grease solvent. The latter compound will make the job much easier, as, after the solvent has been applied and allowed to stand for a time, a vigorous jet of water will wash off the solvent and all the grease and filth. If the dirt is thick and deeply embedded, work the solvent into it with a wire brush.

4 Finally wipe down the exterior of the engine with a rag and only then, when it is quite clean should the dismantling process begin. As the engine is stripped, clean each part in a bath of paraffin or petrol.

5 Never immerse parts with oilways in paraffin, ie; the crankshaft,

but to clean, wipe down carefully with a petrol dampened rag. Oilways can be cleaned out with wire. If an air line is present all parts can be blown dry and the oilways blown through as an added precaution.

6   Re-use of old engine gaskets is false economy and can give rise to oil and water leaks, if nothing worse. To avoid the possibility of trouble after the engine has been reassembled **always** use new gaskets throughout.

7   Do not throw the old gaskets away as it sometimes happens that an immediate replacement cannot be found and the old gasket is then very useful as a template. Hang up the old gaskets as they are removed on a suitable hook or nail.

8   To strip the engine it is best to work from the top down. The sump provides a firm base on which the engine can be supported in an upright position. When the stage where the sump must be removed is reached, the engine can be turned on its side and all other work carried out with it in this position.

9   Wherever possible, replace nuts, bolts and washers fingertight from wherever they were removed. This helps avoid later loss and muddle. If they cannot be replaced then lay them out in such a fashion that it is clear where they came from.

8   Cylinder head - removal

1   *If the engine is in the car,* disconnect the battery, remove the engine compartment lid and the air cleaner.
2   Remove the rocker cover after unscrewing the two securing nuts and their fibre washers.
3   Pull the waterproof cover from the distributor, release the cap clips and remove the cap complete with HT leads.
4   Turn the engine crankshaft until No 1 piston (the rearmost one when installed in the car) is at TDC. This can be established by checking that the timing marks on the oil filter cover and on the timing cover are in alignment and that Nos 1 and 2 valves are fully closed (slight movement discernible at their rocker arms).
5   Now mark the position of the contact end of the rotor arm in relation to the distributor body and also the distributor body in relation to the engine crankcase. Unbolt the distributor clamp plate and remove the distributor.
6   Disconnect the throttle operating rod from the carburettor.
7   Disconnect the fuel pipe which runs between the fuel pump and the carburettor.
8   Unbolt and remove the carburettor. Withdraw the carburettor drip tray.
9   Unscrew and remove the suppressor cap from the spark plugs.
10 Extract all the bolts which secure the top sections of the engine air cooling assembly and lift these sections away.
11 Unbolt the exhaust pipe flanges from both sides of the cylinder head. Pull the flanges slightly from the cylinder head and extract the joint gaskets.
12 Unscrew and remove the rocker pedestal nuts.
13 Lift off the rocker shaft assembly, noting the location of the rocker oil feed pipe.
14 Withdraw the four pushrods and keep them in sequence for refitting in their original positions.
15 Unscrew the four centrally-located cylinder head domed nuts and the four ordinary nuts on the outer edge of the cylinder head.
16 Lift off the cylinder head directly upwards. If it is stuck, tap it carefully with a plastic or wooden mallet.

9   Cam followers (tappets) and cylinder barrels - removal

1   With the cylinder head removed as previously described, extract the pushrod tubes.
2   Extract the circular flexible seals from both ends of the tubes.
3   Extract the cam followers (tappets) keeping them in sequence for refitting in their original positions.
4   Mark which way round each cylinder barrel is fitted and which one is the rearmost and then carefully draw them off the pistons upwards.

10 Sump. pistons/connecting rods - removal

1   If the engine is in the car, drain the engine oil and remove the

cylinder head and barrels, as previously described.
2   Unscrew and remove the sump bolts and remove the sump and gasket.
3   Unbolt the exhaust silencer brackets and remove the silencer assembly.
4   Unbolt and remove the front flange of the generator pulley, extract the shims used for tensioning the drivebelt and remove the belt.
5   Release the generator mounting strap.
6   Unbolt the fan cooling assembly from the engine crankcase and remove the assembly complete with generator. It will be noticed that two of the bolts which secure the fan cooling assembly to the engine are of hollow type. This is a safety feature necessary where the air used for cooling the engine is also used to heat the car interior. Should the cylinder head gasket blow, exhaust gas could leak into the car interior through the heater. A groove is located on the upper surface of the cylinder barrel which connects to these hollow bolts and if exhaust gas is heard or can be felt emerging from these bolts, then the cylinder head gasket must be renewed immediately (photo).
7   Unscrew the connecting rod big-end nuts and remove the big-end cap.
8   Push the connecting rods complete with pistons out of the crankcase through the top face. Note that the connecting rods and their caps are numbered 1 and 2. No 1 is the rearmost, and all numbers face towards the camshaft.

10.6 Engine cooling casing hollow bolt

10.7 Connecting rod and cap numbers

11 Pistons, piston rings, gudgeon pins - removal

1   The pistons have no marks on their crowns and before removing them from their connecting rods, they should be marked with a piece of adhesive tape so that there can be no doubt from which rod they were removed and also which way round on the rod they were fitted.
2   Extract the circlip from both ends of the gudgeon pin and push out the pin. Finger pressure only should be required to do this.
3   To remove the piston rings, start with the top compression ring first. Expand it slightly and slide two or three old feeler blades behind it spacing them at equidistant points of a circle. These will extract the ring from its groove and also provide slides to prevent the lower rings dropping into empty upper grooves as these too are removed.
4   Remove the rings using a twisting motion.

12 Flywheel - removal

1   With the clutch removed as described in Chapter 5, mark the position of the flywheel in relation to the crankshaft mounting flange.
2   Unscrew and remove the flywheel bolts and remove the flywheel. In order to remove the flywheel bolts it will be necessary to prevent the crankshaft rotating. To do this, either place a block of wood between the crankshaft web and the inside of the crankcase or jam the starter ring gear with a large screwdriver.

13 Oil pump, filter, timing gear and camshaft - removal

1   If the engine is in the car, support it on a jack and remove the rear crossmember.
2   Remove the drivebelt, as previously described.
3   Unscrew and remove the cover from the centrifugal oil filter (five bolts).
4   Bend back the locking tab from the nut now exposed within the oil filter housing.
5   Unscrew the nut first having jammed the crankshaft with a piece of wood to prevent it rotating.
6   Extract the thrust washer and the oil thrower.
7   Pull the pulley/oil filter housing straight off the rear of the engine.
8   Unscrew the timing cover nuts and remove the cover.
9   The timing gears and chain are now exposed. Note the timing marks on the gears (dot on camshaft gear and scribed line on crankshaft gear).
10 Unbolt the camshaft gearwheel and remove it complete with crankshaft sprocket and the timing chain.
11 Withdraw the camshaft carefully taking care not to damage the camshaft bearings as the lobes pass through them.

14 Crankshaft and main bearings - removal

1   From the oil pump end of the crankshaft, extract the Woodruff key which secures the timing gear (previously removed).
2   Remove the bolts and countersunk screws which secure the bearing retainer at the oil pump end of the crankshaft. An impact screwdriver will almost certainly be required to remove the screws.
3   Unbolt and remove the bearing retainer at the flywheel end of the crankshaft.
4   Unbolt and remove the oil pick-up tube from inside the crankcase. Note the mounting plate used between the tube flange and the crankcase.
5   Withdraw the crankshaft from the crankcase.

15 Lubrication system and filter maintenance

1   The lubrication system comprises a sump and a gear type oil pump which is mounted within the timing cover and is driven by a dog clutch at the rear end of the camshaft (Fig. 1.5).
2   A large coil spring is used to key the pressure relief valve on its seat and excess pressure causes the valve to lift against the spring pressure.
3   A centrifugal type oil filter is used and this is mounted on the rear

end of the crankshaft.
4   The cover of the filter is removable for routine cleaning and the filter housing acts also as a pulley for the drivebelt which drives the generator and the air cooling fan.
5   Oil is drawn from the sump through the pick-up tube, filtered by the centrifugal type filter and then pressurised by the gear type oil pump and distributed to all the bearings and friction surfaces of the engine.
6   At the intervals specified in 'Routine Maintenance,' unbolt the cover from the centrifugal filter and let any oil residue drain into a container.
7   Clean out both the filter housing and the filter cover. The hard grey deposits will probably require the use of a blunt tool to remove them but take care not to damage the metal surfaces.
8   Scrape off the old gasket and fit a new one, then install the filter cover, tightening the bolts evenly.

16 Crankcase ventilation system - description and maintenance

1   The crankcase ventilation system is simply a hose connecting the rocker cover to the air cleaner so that engine oil fumes and blow-by gases can be extracted from the crankcase and rocker box and be drawn into the inlet manifold where they can be burned during the normal combustion cycle.
2   Refinements incorporated in the system include a valve in the oil filler cap and a backfire eliminator in the connecting hose stub of the filler neck.
3   At the intervals specified in the 'Routine Maintenance' section thoroughly clean the backfire eliminator and check the condition and security of the system hoses. The backfire eliminator is removed simply by extracting it with a pair of pliers (photo).

17 Examination and renovation - general

With the engine stripped down and all parts thoroughly cleaned, it is now time to examine everything for wear. The following items should be checked and where necessary renewed or renovated as described in the following Sections.

18 Crankshaft and main bearings - examination and renovation

1   Use a micrometer to check the main bearing journals for out of round. Check at several different points and if the difference in these measurements exceeds 0.0002 in (0.005 mm) then the crankshaft must be reground and new main bearings fitted (Fig. 1.6).
2   This procedure must also be adopted if there is scoring or scratching on the main bearing journal surfaces.
3   If the crankshaft must be reground, this is obviously a job for your Fiat dealer who will decide how much to grind off and supply the

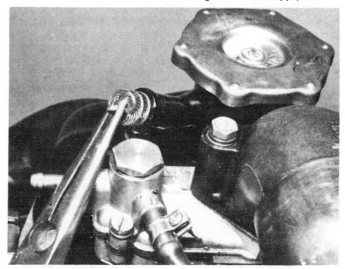

16.3 Extracting anti-backfire device (crankcase vent system)

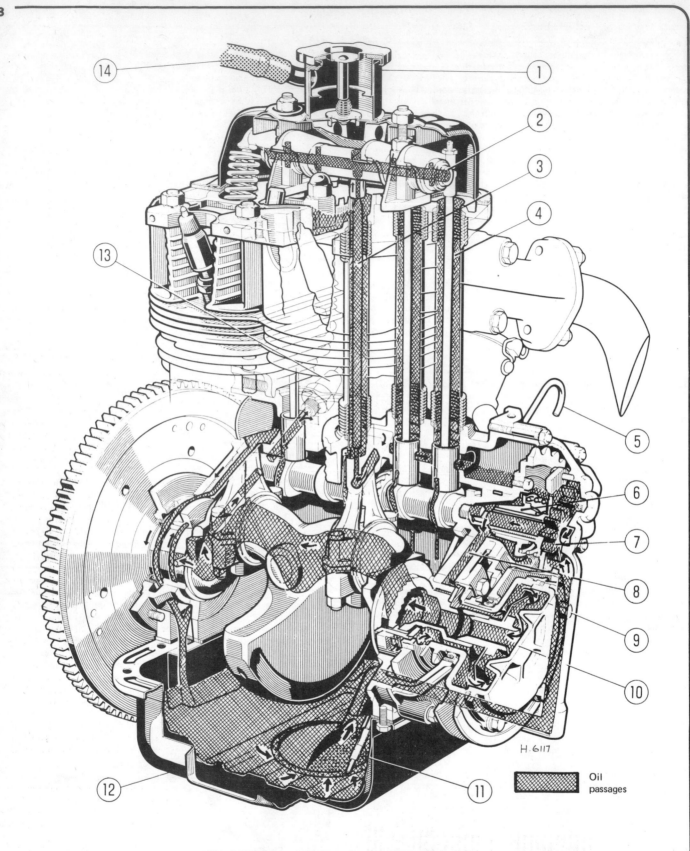

Fig. 1.5. Diagrammatic view of engine lubrication system

1 Oil filler cap
2 Rocker shaft
3 Oil delivery tube to rocker shaft
4 Oil return passages from cylinder head
5 Dipstick
6 Oil pressure relief valve
7 Oil pump gears
8 Oil passage to filter
9 Centrifugal type oil filter
10 Crankshaft oil drilling
11 Oil pick-up tube filter
12 Sump air cooling duct
13 Oil pressure switch
14 Fume extraction pipe to air cleaner

matching undersize main bearings.

4   Crankshaft main bearings are supplied in the appropriate undersizes complete with retainer but leave fitting of bearings to retainers to your Fiat dealer as reaming after heating is necessary.

5   The oil seal in the main bearing assembly at the flywheel end can be renewed if necessary (Section 28).

6   The main bearing assembly at the timing gear end incorporates a piston ring type oil seal and a thrust washer (photo).

7   Whenever the crankshaft has been removed, always check the effectiveness of the oil plug staking (Fig. 1.7).

8   In the centre of the flywheel mounting flange of the crankshaft is located the gearbox input shaft pilot bush. If this is badly worn, extract it by tapping a thread into it, screwing in a bolt and using the bolt to withdraw the bush. Drive in the new bush and apply some grease to its centre.

---

19 Big-end bearings and connecting rods - examination and renovation

1   Check the crankpins for scoring and out of round as for journals described in the preceding Section.

2   New shell bearings are installed simply by extracting the old ones from cap and rod and fitting the new ones.

3   Any wear in the small end bush can only be overcome by pressing out the old bush and pressing in the new one. As the new bush will then require reaming to the specified size, this is a job that is best left to your Fiat dealer.

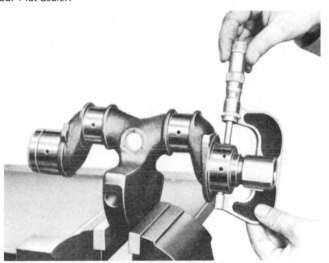

Fig. 1.6. Checking a crankshaft journal

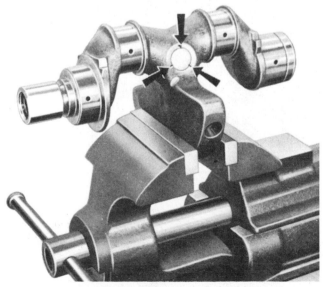

Fig. 1.7. Crankshaft oil plug staking

18.6 Main bearing at timing cover end showing piston ring type oil seal and thrust washer extracted

---

20 Cylinder bores - examination and renovation

1   The cylinder bores must be examined for taper, ovality, scoring and scratches. Start by carefully examining the top of the cylinder bores. If they are at all worn a very slight ridge will be found on the thrust side. This marks the top of the piston ring travel. The owner will have a good indication of the bore wear prior to dismantling the engine, or removing the cylinder head. Excessive oil consumption accompanied by blue smoke from the exhaust is a sure sign of worn cylinder bores and piston rings.

2   Measure the bore diameter just under the ridge with a micrometer and compare it with the diameter at the bottom of the bore, which is not subject to wear. If the difference between the two measurements is more than 0.0008 in (0.02 mm) then it will be necessary to fit special pistons and rings or to have the cylinders rebored and fit oversize pistons. If no micrometer is available remove the rings from a piston and place the piston in each bore in turn about ¾ in (19.05 mm) below the top of the bore. If an 0.0012 in (0.03 mm) thick feeler gauge slid between the piston and cylinder wall requires less than a pull of between 2.2 and 5.5 lbs (1 and 2.5 kg) to withdraw it, using a spring balance, then remedial action must be taken. Oversize pistons are available as listed in the Specifications.

3   These are accurately machined to just below the indicated measurements so as to provide correct running clearances in bores bored out to the exact oversize dimensions.

4   If the bores are slightly worn but not so badly worn as to justify reboring them, then special oil control rings and pistons can be fitted which will restore compression and stop the engine burning oil. Several different types are available and the manufacturer's instructions concerning their fitting must be followed closely.

5   If new pistons or rings are being fitted and the bores have not been reground, it is essential to slightly roughen the hard glaze on the sides of the bores with fine glass paper so the new piston rings will have a chance to bed in properly.

---

21 Pistons and piston rings - examination and renovation

1   If the original pistons are to be refitted, carefully remove the piston rings as described in Section 11.

2   Clean the grooves and rings free from carbon, taking care not to scratch the aluminium surfaces of the pistons.

3   If new rings are considered necessary, consult your local engineering firm as to the availability of a set of rings with the top one 'stepped'. This 'step' will avoid the ridge which occurs near the top of the bore after a high mileage and will prevent the new ring being broken. Be guided by the advice of the engineering firm, as the fitting of new rings to an otherwise worn piston and bore can only be a very temporary cure to the inevitable rebore!

4   Before fitting the rings to the pistons, push each ring in turn down to the bottom of its respective cylinder bore (use an inverted piston to do this so that the ring is kept square in its bore) and then measure the piston ring end gap.
5   This gap should be as shown in the Specifications, otherwise carefully grind the end faces of the ring.
6   Each piston ring should now be tested in its respective groove for side clearance. Use a feeler blade to do this and compare the clearances with those listed in the Specifications (Fig. 1.8).
7   Where the side clearance is excessive, renew the piston as it will be the grooves that will have worn.
8   Where necessary a piston ring which is slightly tight in its groove may be rubbed down holding it perfectly squarely on an oilstone or a sheet of fine emery cloth laid on a piece of plate glass. Excessive tightness can only be rectified by having the grooves machined out.
9   The gudgeon pin should be a push fit with the fingers in both the piston and small end bush of the connecting rod. Any slackness must be rectified by renewal of the small end bush or piston or both.

22 Camshaft and cam-followers (tappets) - examination and renovation

1   The camshaft runs directly in the crankcase. Any wear in the bearing surfaces will seriously affect the engine oil pressure.
2   Where any wear is found in the camshaft journals after measuring their diameters with a micrometer and comparing the dimensions with those given in the Specifications, the camshaft must be renewed. This action will also have to be taken if the camshaft journals are found to be out of round.
3   If the camshaft bores in the crankcase are found to be worn, then the crankcase will have to be renewed.
4   It may be possible to have the crankcase and camshaft built up by metal spraying or a similar technique and then refinished to provide the specified running clearances but check the cost of new components against the charge for this type of work first.
5   Wear in the camshaft lobes can only be satisfactorily measured with a dial gauge. Use this to compare the lobe lift figures with those specified which are: inlet and exhaust - 0.244 in (6.2 mm).
6   Any wear in the lobes or skew gear can only be overcome by renewal of the camshaft.
7   If the cam followers are slack in their crankcase bores, oversize cam followers can be fitted if the bores are first reamed out. This is a job best left to your Fiat dealer. Oversizes supplied 0.0019 to 0.0039 in (0.05 to 0.10 mm).

23 Timing components - examination and renovation

1   Examine all the sprocket teeth for wear or 'hooked' appearance and renew if necessary.
2   Wash the timing chain, thoroughly in paraffin and examine for wear or stretch. If the chain is supported at both ends so that the rollers are vertical then a worn chain will take on a deeply bowed appearance while an unworn one will dip slightly at its centre point.

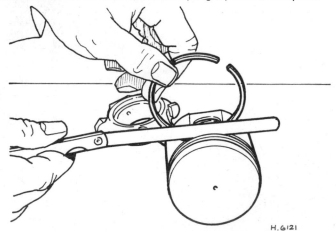

H. G121

Fig. 1.8. Checking piston ring side clearance

3   The timing chain incorporates self-tensioning side plates on one side of the chain. These tend to fly out in operation due to centrifugal force and so keep the chain constantly tensioned.

24 Valves and valve guides - servicing

1   Each valve should be removed from the cylinder head using the following method.
2   Compress each spring using a valve spring compressor, until the split collets can be removed. Release the compressor slowly, remove it and then remove the retainer, valve springs, and the valve spring seat. Finally withdraw the valve from its guide (photos).
3   If, when the valve spring compressor is screwed down, the valve spring retaining cap refuses to free to expose the split collet, do not continue to screw down on the compressor as there is a likelihood of bending the valve stem.
4   Gently tap the top of the tool directly over the cap with a light hammer. This will free the cap. To avoid the compressor jumping off the valve spring retaining cap when it is tapped, hold the compressor firmly in position with one hand.
5   Slide the rubber oil control seal off the end of each inlet valve stem and then drop out each valve through the combustion chamber . Later engines do not have oil seals on the valve stems.
6   It is essential that the valves are kept in their correct sequences unless they are so badly worn that they are to be renewed. If they are going to be kept and used again, place them in a sheet of card having holes numbered 1 to 4 corresponding with the relative positions the valves were in when fitted. Also keep the valve springs, washers etc in the correct order.
7   Examine the heads of the valves for pitting and burning, especially the heads of the exhaust valves. The valve seatings should be examined at the same time. If the pitting on valve and seat is very slight the marks can be removed by grinding the seats and valves together with coarse, and then fine, valve grinding paste.
8   Where bad pitting has occured to the valve seats it will be necessary to recut them and fit new valves. Cut the valve seat in three stages as indicated, using first a 45° cutter then one of 20° and finally a 75° cutter to give a seat contact width of between 0.71 and 0.83 in (1.8 and 2.1 mm) (Fig. 1.9). In practice it is very seldom that the seats are so badly worn that they require recutting. Normally, it is the valve that is too badly worn to use again and the owner can easily purchase a new set of valves and match them to the seats by grinding.
9   Valve grinding is carried out as follows. Smear a trace of coarse carborundum paste on the seat face and apply a suction grinder tool to the valve head. With a semi-rotary motion, grind the valve head to its seat, lifting the valve occasionally to redistribute the grinding paste. When a dull matt, even surface finish is produced on both the valve seat and the valve, wipe off the paste and repeat the process with fine carborundum paste, lifting and turning the valve to distribute the paste as before. A light spring placed under the valve head will greatly ease this operation. When a smooth unbroken ring of light grey matt finish is produced, on both valve and valve seat faces, the grinding operation is completed.
10 Scrape away all carbon from the valve head and the valve stem. Carefully clean away every trace of grinding compound, taking great care to leave none in the ports or in the valve guides. Clean the valves and valve seats with a paraffin soaked rag, then with a dry rag, and finally, if an air line is available, blow the valves, valve guides and valve ports clean.
11 Wear in the valve guides can best be checked by inserting a new valve and testing for rocking movement in all directions. The clearance between the guide and valve stem must not exceed 0.003 in (0.08 mm).
12 Reassemble the valves, springs and collets in reverse order.
13 Valve guides are an interference fit in the cylinder head and they may be renewed using a suitable mandrel as a drift. New guides are supplied in (outside diameter) oversizes to provide the correct interference fit.
14 Install the valve guide in accordance with the diagram (Fig. 1.10).

25 Cylinder head - decarbonising and examination

1   With the cylinder head removed, use a blunt scraper to remove all trace of carbon and deposits from the combustion spaces and ports.

Remember that the cylinder head is aluminium alloy and can be damaged easily during the decarbonising operations. Scrape the cylinder head free from scale or old pieces of gasket or jointing compound. Clean the cylinder head by washing it in paraffin and take particular care to pull a piece of rag through the ports and cylinder head bolt holes. Any dirt remaining in these recesses may well drop onto the gasket or cylinder block mating surface as the cylinder head is lowered into position and could lead to a gasket leak after reassembly is complete.

2   With the cylinder head clean, test for distortion if a history of gas leakage has been apparent. Carry out this test using a straight edge and feeler gauges or a piece of plate glass. If the surface shows any warping in excess of 0.0039 in (0.1 mm) then the cylinder head will have to be resurfaced which is a job for a specialist engineering company.

3   Clean the pistons and top of the cylinder bores. If the pistons are still in the block then it is essential that great care is taken to ensure that no carbon gets into the cylinder bores as this could scratch the cylinder walls or cause damage to the piston and rings. To ensure this does not happen, first turn the crankshaft so that both the pistons are at the top of their bores.

4   Before scraping the carbon from the piston crowns, press grease into the gap between the cylinder wall and the two pistons. With a blunt scraper carefully scrape away the carbon from the piston crown, taking great care not to scratch the aluminium. Also scrape away the carbon from the surrounding lip of the cylinder wall. When all carbon

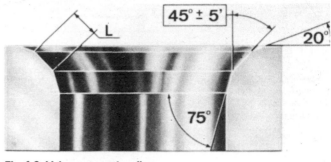
Fig. 1.9. Valve seat cutting diagram
1st - 45°   2nd - 20°   3rd - 75°
Seat width (L) is between 0.071 and 0.083 in (1.8 and 2.1 mm)

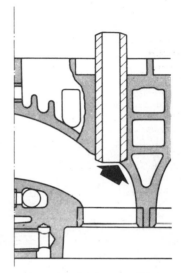
Fig. 1.10. Valve guide installation diagram (note flush fitting at bottom chamfer (arrowed)

24.2a Compressing a valve spring

24.2b Removing valve spring retainer

24.2c Removing an outer valve spring

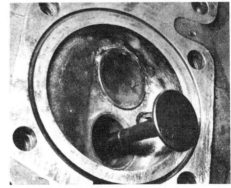
24.2d Removing a valve spring seat

24.2e Removing a valve

has been removed scrape away the grease which will now be contaminated with carbon particles, taking care not to press any into the bores. To assist prevention of carbon build-up the piston crown can be polished with a metal polish.

26 Flywheel - examination and renovation

1   Check the clutch friction lining mating face of the flywheel. If it is grooved or scored, then the flywheel must be renewed.

2   If the starter ring gear is worn or the teeth are clipped, a new ring gear can be fitted using the following method.

3   Either split the ring with a cold chisel after making a cut with a

hacksaw blade between two teeth, or use a soft headed hammer (not steel) to knock the ring off, striking it evenly and alternatively at equally spaced points. Take great care not to damage the flywheel during this process.

4   Heat the new ring in either an electric oven to about 200°C (392°F) or immerse in a pan of boiling oil.

5   Hold the ring at this temperature for five minutes and then quickly fit it to the flywheel.

6   The ring should be tapped gently down onto its register and left to cool naturally when the contraction of the metal on cooling will ensure that it is a secure and permanent fit. Great care must be taken not to overheat the ring (indicated by the ring turning light metallic blue) as if this happens the temper of the ring will be lost.

27 Crankcase - examination and renovation

1   Inspect the crankcase for cracks particularly of the stud and bolt holes.
2   Renew any studs which have stripped or damaged threads.
3   Inspect the security of the Welch plugs. Renew any that are suspect.

28 Oil seals - renewal

1   At time of major overhaul, renew the oil seals as a matter of routine.
2   Drive out the timing cover oil seal using a piece of tubing as a drift and install the new one by the same method. Apply grease to the seal lips after fitting (Fig. 1.11).
3   Renew the oil seal in the crankshaft main bearing retainer (flywheel end) in the same way (Fig. 1.12 and photo).

29 Oil pump - overhaul

1   With the timing cover removed, the oil pump can be dismantled if necessary.
2   A compressor will be needed to compress the pressure relief valve spring so that the retaining circlip can be extracted. A valve spring compressor used with a suitable adaptor might serve the purpose, otherwise bolt a flat bar across the timing cover flanges and use this as a leverage point to depress the relief valve and in turn, the spring (Figs. 1.13, 1.14 and 1.15).
3   The components of the oil pump may now be removed and the cover unbolted.
4   Check the teeth of the gears for wear or chipping and renew them if evident.
5   Measure the length of the spring. This should be between 1.38 and 1.46 in (35.2 - 37.2 mm) in its free state. If it is shorter, renew it.
6   Reassemble the pump by reversing the dismantling operations.

30 Rocker gear and pushrods - examination and renovation

1   Any wear in the rocker shaft or arms can only be rectified by renewal of the components.
2   If the circlips are extracted and the rocker arms are removed from the rocker shaft, keep all components in strict sequence so that they can be installed in their original positions.
3   Check the pushrods for distortion. If any of them appear to be bent, renew them.

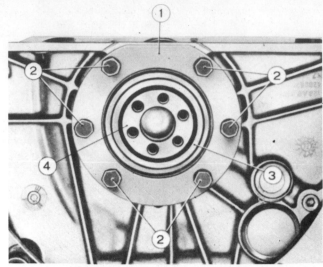

Fig. 1.12. Crankshaft main bearing retainer(1) Securing bolts(2) Oil seal(3) and Crankshaft flywheel mounting flange (4)

Fig. 1.13. Oil pump within timing cover

1 Timing cover	4 Circlip
2 Pump securing bolts	5 Oil pressure relief valve
3 Pump drive shaft	6 Relief valve spring

Fig. 1.11. Timing cover (1) and oil seal (2)

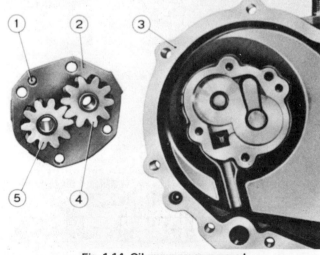

Fig. 1.14. Oil pump cover removed

1 Locating dowel	4 Driven gear
2 Pump cover	5 Drive gear and shaft
3 Timing cover	

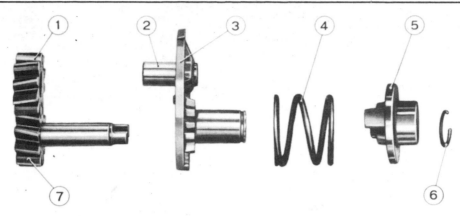

Fig. 1.15. Exploded view of the oil pump

1 *Driven gear*	3 *Cover*	5 *Relief valve*	7 *Drive gear and shaft*
2 *Shaft*	4 *Spring*	6 *Circlip*	

31 Engine reassembly - general

1   To ensure maximum life with minimum trouble from a re-built engine, not only must everything be correctly assembled but everything must be spotlessly clean, all the oilways must be clear, locking washers and spring washers must always be fitted where indicated and all bearing and other working surfaces must be thoroughly lubricated during assembly.

2   Before assembly begins renew any bolts or studs the threads of which are in any way damaged and whenever possible use new spring washers.

3   Apart from your normal tools, a supply of clean rag, an oil can filled with engine oil, a new supply of assorted spring washers, a set of new gaskets and a torque wrench, should be collected together.

32 Crankshaft and main bearings - refitting

1   Pass the crankshaft into the crankcase and push it as far as possible through one of the main bearing holes, then bring it back so that it rests in the main bearing holes of the crankcase. The flywheel mounting flange will obviously be towards the bellhousing (photo).

2   Lubricate the main bearing surfaces liberally and install the front and rear main bearings. A gasket is used on the main bearing flange at the flywheel end only (photos).

3   The main bearing retainers will only fit one way as they have a flat on one side which aligns with the sump flange.

4   Install the bearing retaining bolts and screws and tighten to the specified torque.

5   Install the Woodruff key to the end of the crankshaft (photo).

28.3 Main bearing retainer (flywheel end) showing oil seal

32.1 Installing the crankshaft

32.2a Installing the main bearing retainer (timing gear end)

32.2b Installing bolts and screws to main bearing retainer (timing gear end)

32.5 Woodruff key installed to end of crankshaft

33 Camshaft, timing gear, filter and oil pump - refitting

1   Lubricate the camshaft bearings liberally and install the camshaft into the crankcase (photo).
2   Temporarily fit the camshaft and crankshaft chain sprockets to the ends of the camshaft and crankshaft. The camshaft sprocket can only be fitted in one position as the bolt holes are offset.
3   Turn the sprockets until the dot on the edge of the camshaft sprocket is in alignment with the scribed line on the crankshaft sprocket and an imaginary line drawn through the sprocket centres (photo).
4   Remove the sprockets and keeping them in this relative position, engage their teeth within the loop of the timing chain. The tensioner plates of the timing chain must be furthest from the crankcase (photo).
5   Install the two sprockets complete with chain without moving the previously set position of the camshaft or crankshaft. Some slight re-adjustment of the sprockets within the chain may be necessary to align the camshaft sprocket bolt holes and yet maintain the alignment of the timing marks.
6   Fit the camshaft sprocket bolts, tighten to the specified torque and bend up the tabs of the lockplates.
7   Install the timing cover using a new gasket. Make sure that the oil pump mates correctly with the drive dog on the end of the camshaft as the timing cover is offered into position (photos).
8   Push the pulley/oil filter assembly into position on the end of the crankshaft, fit the lockplate and hollow bolt and tighten to the specified torque. Jam the crankshaft web with a block of wood to prevent it turning while the bolt is being tightened. Bend up the tab of the lockplate (photos).
9   Fit the oil filter cover using a new 'O' ring oil seal (photo).

34 Flywheel - refitting

1   Install the flywheel to the mounting flange on the crankshaft so that the marks made before removal are in alignment.
2   Install and tighten the securing bolts to the specified torque wrench setting. To prevent the flywheel turning as the bolts are tightened, jam the crankshaft with a block of wood (photo).

35 Pistons, piston rings and gudgeon pins - reassembly

1   If the piston has been removed from the connecting rod, refit it so that the larger offset and the numbers on the connecting rod will be towards the camshaft when installed (Fig. 1.16).
2   Push in the gudgeon pin using finger-pressure only and then fit new securing circlips (photo).
3   Fit the slotted oil control ring to the lowest groove of the piston followed by the plain oil control ring (stepped on its lower edge) and then the chrome-plated compression ring. This is marked 'TOP' on its upper face.
4   When the rings are installed, stagger their end-gaps at equidistant points of a circle to avoid gap alignment which might cause gas blow-by.

36 Pistons/connecting rods and sump - refitting

1   Fit the shell bearings to the connecting rod and to the big-end cap. Make sure that the backs of the shells are quite clean also the recesses into which they fit. Lubricate the shell bearing surfaces (photo).
2   Pass the connecting rod/piston assembly into the crankcase through the hole in the top of the crankcase (photo).
3   Engage the connecting rod with the crankpin of the crankshaft, install the big-end cap and screw on and tighten the securing nuts to the specified torque (photos). The numbers on the rod and cap must face towards the camshaft. Remember No 1 rod and piston are in the rearmost position in the engine.
4   Install the second piston/rod assembly in a similar manner.
5   Install the oil pump pick-up tube within the crankcase (photo).
6   Fit a new sump gasket and install the sump. Make sure that the oil drain slots in the sump gasket are correctly located (photo).

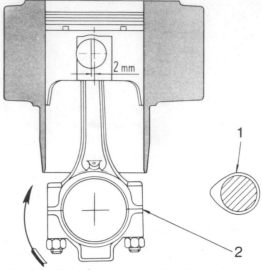

Fig. 1.16. Piston/connecting rod installation diagram

1   Camshaft   *2   Rod and cap numbers*

37 Cylinder barrels, cam followers (tappets) and pushrod tubes - refitting

1   Oil the piston rings liberally and fit narrow piston ring compressors. Install the barrel lower gaskets to the crankcase (photos).
2   Make sure that the piston and compressor are sitting quite squarely on the top of the crankcase and then lower the cylinder barrel onto the piston. Make sure that the correct barrel is installed to its respective piston and it is fitted the correct way round with its bore liberally oiled.
3   Tap the barrel sharply down with the palm of the hand to displace the compressor and engage the lower end of the barrel with the crankcase. If the engine is out of the car, it may be preferred to install the pistons into the barrels and then insert the big-ends of the connecting rods into the crankcase and lower the complete piston/barrel assembly onto the securing studs. This method is not recommended if the engine is still in position in the car.
4   Repeat the operations on the second piston (photo).
5   Insert the cam followers (tappets) in their original positions (photo).
6   Install the pushrod tubes using new seals (photos).
7   Install the rocker oil feed pipe (photo).

38 Cylinder head - installation

1   Make sure that the cylinder head and cylinder barrel mating surfaces are absolutely clean.
2   Position a new gasket on the barrels, making sure that the word 'ALTO' is visible on the top face and then lower the cylinder head into position (photos).
3   Screw on the cylinder head nuts (domed ones in the centre) and tighten to the specified torque in the sequence shown in Fig. 1.17 (photo).
4   When installing the cylinder head, make sure that the pushrod tube seals engage correctly at top and bottom ends of the tubes.
5   Release all the rocker arm adjuster screws, install the pushrods in their original fitted sequence and then install the rocker shaft assembly. Make sure that the rocker oil feed pipe engages correctly.
6   Tighten the rocker pedestal bolts to the specified torque.
7   Adjust the valve clearances, as described in Section 39, and then fit the rocker cover using a new gasket. If the carburettor has yet to be installed, do not fit the rocker cover as one of the carburettor flange bolts is difficult to tighten with the cover on.
8   If the operations described in this Section are being carried out with the engine in the car, reverse the work described in paragraphs 1 to 11 of Section 8, but use new flange gaskets at the exhaust pipe connections to the cylinder head.

33.1 Installing the camshaft

33.3 Timing sprocket alignment marks

33.4 Timing chain and sprockets correctly located

33.6 Camshaft timing sprocket bolts and lock plates installed

33.7a Interior of timing cover

33.7b Oil pump driven dog

33.8a Installing oil filter/pulley assembly

33.8b Tightening oil filter/pulley centre nut

33.9 Installing oil filter cover with 'O' ring seal

34.2 Tightening a flywheel bolt

35.2 Installing a gudgeon pin

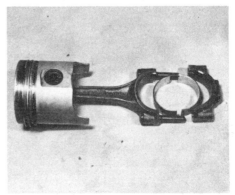
36.1 Piston/connecting rod with shell bearings

36.2 Installing a piston/connecting rod assembly

36.3a Fitting a big-end bearing cap

36.3b Tightening a big-end bearing cap nut

36.5 Installing oil pump pick-up tube

36.6 Installing the sump

37.1a Piston ring clamp in position

37.1b Cylinder barrel with base sealing gasket

37.4 Installing cylinder barrel to piston

37.5 Inserting a cam follower into crankcase

37.6a Push-rod tube bottom oil seals

37.6b Push-rod tubes installed

37.7 Rocker oil feed pipe installed

38.2a Cylinder head gasket upper surface

38.2b Installing the cylinder head

38.3 Tightening a cylinder head nut

38.5a Installing a push-rod

38.5b Installing the rocker shaft assembly

39.3 Checking and adjusting a valve clearance

Fig. 1.17. Cylinder head nut tightening sequence diagram

3 Now check the clearance between the ends of the valve stems and the rocker arm **of the other two valves which are not 'in balance'** using a feeler blade (photo). The clearance for inlet valves is 0.008 in (0.20 mm) and for exhaust valves 0.010 in (0.25 mm). Numbering from the rear of the car, valves are 1 and 4 exhaust, 2 and 3 inlet.
4 Where adjustment is required, slacken the rocker arm adjuster screw locknut and turn the adjuster screw until the feeler blade is a stiff sliding fit. Retighten the locknut without disturbing the adjustment.
5 Rotate the crankshaft and repeat the operations on the remaining two valves.
6 The crankshaft can be turned in several different ways. Always remove the spark plugs to prevent compression making the crankshaft harder to turn. If the engine is in the car, engage top gear and push the car forward while an assistant watches the position of the rocker arms. If the engine is out of the car, grip the pulley/oil filter housing and turn it with the hands, alternatively, apply a ring spanner to one of the flywheel bolts (if the clutch has been removed) and use this. Whether the engine is in or out of the car, it is not considered advisable to turn the crankshaft by applying a spanner to one of the oil filter cover bolts as it may shear.

40 Engine - final reassembly before installation

1 Install the fan cooling assemblies to both sides of the engine (Chapter 2).
2 Install the exhaust silencer assembly (Chapter 3).
3 Install the generator (Chapter 10). Adjust the drivebelt (Chapter 2).
4 Install the fuel pump, carburettor and air cleaner (Chapter 3).
5 Install the distributor (Chapter 4).
6 Install the clutch mechanism (Chapter 5).

39 Valve clearances - adjustment

1 The valve clearances should be checked and adjusted only when the engine is cold.
2 Turn the crankshaft until two of the valves of one cylinder are 'in balance'. This means that any slight movement of the crankshaft in either direction will cause either the inlet or exhaust valve of the pair to start opening.

41 Engine - installation

1   Mount the engine on a timber support placed under the exhaust silencer and the base of the left-hand fan cooling assembly, then position it on a trolley jack.
2   Install the engine by engaging it with the clutch bellhousing. The gearbox input shaft will only pass through the spines of the clutch driven plate hub if the driven plate has been correctly centralised, as described in Chapter 5.
3   Install the rear crossmember, making sure that the earth strap is reconnected under one of the securing nuts.
4   Reconnect the engine rear mounting.
5   Install the bellhousing to engine bolts and then withdraw the trolley jack.
6   *Working under the car* reconnect the car interior heater duct, the starter motor operating cable and electrical leads.
7   Refit the lower cover to the clutch bellhousing.
8   Refit the engine under tray and check that the sump plug is tight.
9   *Working within the engine compartment* reconnect the rear licence plate lamp leads.
10 Install the heat shield above the exhaust silencer.
11 Reconnect the trunking which supplies cooling air to the engine fan unit.
12 Reconnect the fuel pipe which runs between the fuel pump and the carburettor. On later models, reconnect the fuel return pipe.
13 Reconnect the accelerator and choke controls to the carburettor.
14 Reconnect the lead to the oil pressure switch.
15 Reconnect the LT and HT leads to the ignition coil and check that the spark plugs have been tightened and the leads correctly connected to them after the plug suppressors have been screwed into place.
16 Reconnect the leads to the generator.
17 Refill the engine with the correct quantity and grade of engine oil.
18 Reconnect the battery negative lead.

42 Initial start-up after major overhaul

1   Check the engine compartment for tools and rags which have not been removed.
2   If a number of new engine internal components have been installed, then the idling speed screw should be turned so that the engine will have a slightly increased slow-running speed to offset the stiffness of the new parts.
3   Start the engine and check for oil or exhaust gas leaks.
4   The car should now be run to normal operating temperature and the carburettor and ignition settings checked as described in Chapter 3 and 4, respectively.
5   Treat the engine as a new unit for the first few hundred miles until the new components have run in.
6   After the first 1,000 miles (1,600 km) check the torque wrench setting of the cylinder head nuts and check and adjust the valve clearances while the engine is cold. Renew the engine oil at approximately the same mileage while the engine is hot.

43 Fault diagnosis - engine

Symptom	Reason/s
Engine will not turn over when starter switch is operated	Flat battery. Bad battery connections. Bad connections at starter motor. Starter motor jammed. Starter motor defective.
Engine turns over normally but fails to start	No spark at plugs. No fuel reaching engine. Too much fuel reaching the engine (flooding)
Engine starts but runs unevenly and misfires	Ignition and/or fuel system faults. Incorrect valve clearances. Burnt out valves. Worn out piston rings.
Lack of power	Ignition and/or fuel system faults. Incorrect valve clearances. Burnt out valves. Worn out piston rings.
Excessive oil consumption	Oil leaks from crankshaft rear oil seal, timing cover gasket and oil seal, rocker cover gasket, oil filter gasket, sump gasket, sump plug washer. Worn piston rings or cylinder bores resulting in oil being burnt by engine. Worn valve guides and/or defective inlet valve stem seals.
Excessive mechanical noise from engine	Wrong valve to rocker clearances. Worn crankshaft bearings. Worn cylinder (piston slap). Slack or worn timing chain and sprockets.

Note: When investigating starting and uneven running faults do not be tempted into snap diagnosis. Start from the beginning of the check procedure and follow it through. It will take less time in the long run. Poor performance from an engine in terms of power and economy is not normally diagnosed quickly. In any event the ignition and fuel systems must be checked first before assuming any further investigation needs to be made.

Chapter 2 Cooling and heating systems

Contents

Specifications

System type	Air cooling by belt driven fan and engine outer casings. Interior heating by exhausted air from engine cooling system.
Drivebelt tension	¼ to ½ in (6.35 to 12.7 mm) deflection at centre of top run of belt.

Torque wrench settings

	lb f ft	Nm
Fan to dynamo shaft nut	25	35
Dynamo pulley nuts	25	35

1 General description

1 The engine is cooled by ample finning and forced draught generated by a fan driven from the end of the dynamo armature shaft.
2 When the engine is running, air is drawn in through two grilles located one on each side of the engine compartment and pressurised by the fan which is enclosed in a casing which in turn is attached to the engine (Fig. 2.1 and photo).
3 The air having cooled the engine and absorbed some of its heat, then passes out from the casing on the opposite side of the engine.
4 The volume of air expelled is restricted by a flap valve which is connected to a thermostat. This arrangement maintains the engine operating temperature at its most efficient level by continuously adjusting the speed of airflow over the engine.
5 Warm air being discharged from the engine cooling casing is utilised for warming the interior of the car (Fig. 2.2).
6 Warm air for the car interior is fed through a duct which has outlets also at the base of the windscreen for demisting and defrosting purposes. This duct is used to distribute and blend fresh air which is drawn in from a front mounted intake. This fresh air can be used as a fresh air ventilation system independently of the heater.
7 Stale air from the car interior is exhausted through grilles on the body pillars against which the doors close.

2 Heating and ventilation controls - operation

1 The main control for the admission of heated air to the car interior is located on the centre floor tunnel within the rear passenger compartment.
2 Looking down on this lever, moving it fully clockwise opens the warm air inlet valve fully while turning it anticlockwise closes it.
3 Immediately below the centre of the fascia panel is the air distribution and control panel. The operation of these controls is described in the caption to Fig. 2.3.

3 Fan cooling casings - removal, dismantling and installation

1 Release the spring clips on the air cleaner cover and remove the connecting pipes which run between the air cleaner and the intake manifold.
2 Remove the cover from the air cleaner and extract the air cleaner element.
3 Disconnect the accelerator cable swivel from the bracket on the cooling housing upper panel. This is achieved by extracting the circlip from the base of the swivel.

1.2 Engine cooling air intake grille

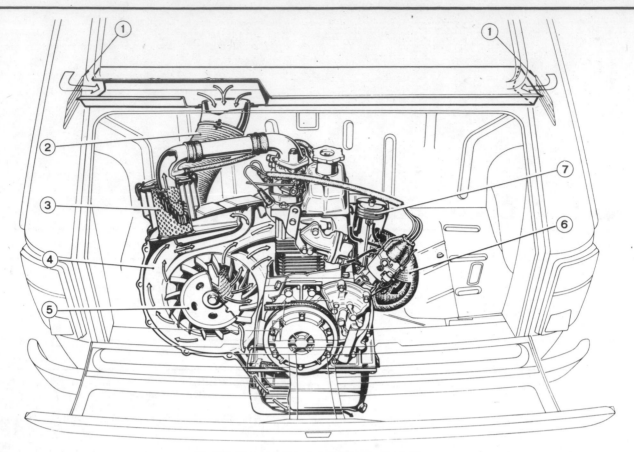

Fig. 2.1. Diagram of engine cooling air circulation

1 Air inlet grilles	3 Air cleaner element	5 Fan	7 Warm air outlet thermostat
2 Air inlet ducting	4 Fan cooling casing	6 Car interior heater hose	and baffle valve
		connection	

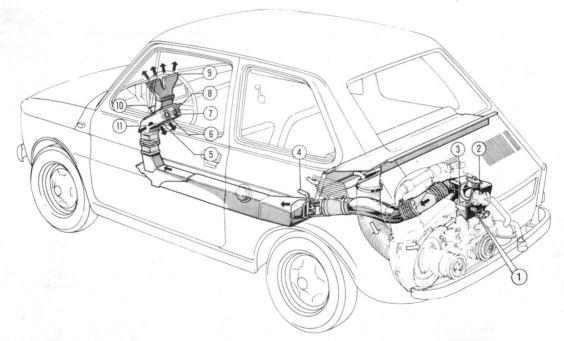

Fig. 2.2. Car interior heating and ventilation system diagram

1 Hollow bolt for gasket blow safety
   device
2 Warm air outlet thermostat
3 Warm air outlet baffle

4 Main heater warm air inlet valve
5 Centre air outlet
6 Upper vents
7 Air distribution control
8 Fresh air control

9 Demister outlets
10 Fresh air intake (for heater/
   ventilator
11 Side air outlet

4   Disconnect the throttle link rod and the return spring.

5   Unbolt and remove the upper panel of the fan cooling casing. This will come away with the air cleaner body which is an integral part of it (photo).

6   Unbolt and remove the front flange of the pulley on the dynamo. Retain any shims carefully and detach the drivebelt (photo).

7   Disconnect the leads from the dynamo terminals.

8   Unscrew the mounting strap bolt at the base of the dynamo, pull out the upper strap pin. Note the earth strap located under the strap bolt (photo).

9   Extract the bolts which hold the fan cooling casing to the engine and remove the casing complete with dynamo. Release the air inlet duct from the back of the casing as it is withdrawn (photo), also the outlet duct for the car interior heater (photo).

10 The dynamo can now be removed from the fan cooling casing if required by first unscrewing the nut which secures the fan to the end of the dynamo armature shaft and then unscrewing the two nuts which secure the dynamo mounting flange to the fan cooling casing (photos). Take care as the dynamo is withdrawn, not to lose the small Woodruff key which secures the fan to the dynamo shaft (Fig. 2.4). Withdraw the pulley shield.

11 To extract the fan, split the fan cooling casing by unscrewing the bolts which secure both halves of the casing together (photos).

12 The section of the cooling casing which contains the air temperature regulating thermostat and baffle valve can be removed from the opposite side of the engine simply by unscrewing the securing bolts (photo).

13 An essential part of the air cooling arrangement is the air passage assembly on the base of the sump. Always take great care to spread the load by using a thick piece of wood when jacking up the engine under the sump (Fig. 2.5).

14 If the fan cooling casing was removed complete with dynamo and the dynamo has not been detached, it can be installed in the same way, making sure that the plastic locating dowel peg at the base of the dynamo engages correctly in the hole in the dynamo support cradle of the engine crankcase and that the pulley shield is refitted (photo).

15 If the dynamo has been detached from the fan casing after removal, it is recommended that the casing is refitted first, without the dynamo.

16 In either event, make sure that the hollow bolts which are located at the top of both the left-hand and right-hand cooling casings are correctly positioned for the reason described in Chapter 1, Section 10.

17 Refit and adjust the drivebelt, as described in Section 5.

18 When refitting the air cleaner element, make sure that the open end of the element is uppermost.

Fig. 2.4. Method of holding dynamo pulley while unscrewing fan securing nut

1 Pulley	3 Fan to dynamo armature shaft nut (exposed after disconnecting air inlet ducting)
2 Tool	4 Fan

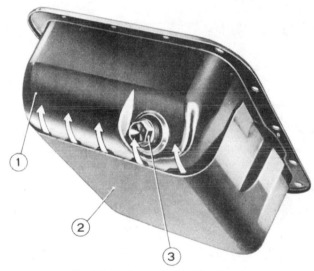

Fig. 2.5. Engine sump cooling air passages

1 Sump	2 Air deflector casing	3 Drain plug

4   Cooling air thermostat - testing and renewal

1   Any fault developing in the thermostat or baffle valve which are located in the cooling casing on the right-hand side of the engine may cause overheating or conversely cool running. Either condition will adversely affect engine performance and fuel economy (photo).

2   Where these symptoms occur, remove the right-hand cooling casing, as described in the preceding Section.

3   To test the operation of the thermostat, immerse it in hot water or hot air at specified temperature levels. If the thermostat is in good condition and the baffle valve and linkage are not seized or broken, operation should be in line with the following temperature ranges:

Valve begins to open	154 to 163°F (68 to 73°C)
Valve fully open	188 to 199°F (87 to 93°C)

4   If the components are found to be faulty as a result of the test, the thermostat can be removed after bending down the tab of the lockplate, and unscrewing the retaining nut and disconnecting the relay linkage.

5   The baffle valve assembly can be removed after extracting the two securing screws.

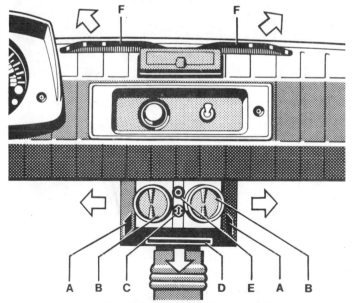

Fig. 2.3. Heating and ventilation controls

A   Side outlets
B   Upper swivel vents
C   Air distribution control (IN to demister outlets F, OUT to all outlets)
D   Centre outlet
E   Fresh air control (IN closed OUT open)

3.5 Removing top cover from fan cooling casing

3.6 Fan pulley adjustment shims

3.8 Dynamo mounting strap bolt and earth strap

3.9a Engine cooling air inlet duct

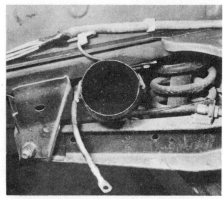

3.9b Car interior heater duct from engine cooling casing

3.10a Dynamo flange mounting nuts

3.10b Fan to dynamo shaft securing nut

3.10c Removing dynamo from fan cooling casing

3.11a Fan cooling casing joint bolts

3.11b Fan viewed from above with top cover removed

3.12 Removing the right-hand engine cooling casing

3.14 Dynamo plastic locating dowel peg

4.1 Fan cooling casing thermostat and link rod

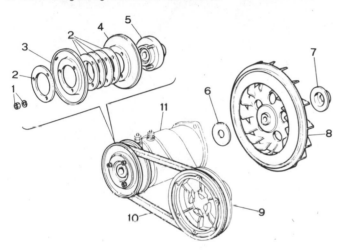

Fig. 2.6. Fan and dynamo pulley components

1	Nut and spring washer	8	Engine cooling fan
2	Adjustment shims	9	Drive pulley (part of
3	Pulley front flange		centrifugal oil filter)
4	Pulley rear flange	10	Drive belt
5	Pulley mounting hub	11	Dynamo
6	Plain washer		
7	Spacer		

5 Fan/dynamo drivebelt - adjustment or renewal

1 Adjustment or renewal of the drivebelt is carried out by altering the effective width of the dynamo pulley groove by the extraction or insertion of shims (Fig. 2.6).

2 The correct tension of the drivebelt is between ¼ and ½ in (6.35 and 12.7 mm) when the centre of the upper run of the belt is depressed with the thumb (Fig. 2.7).

3 To fit a new belt or to adjust the tension, unbolt the front flange of the dynamo pulley.

4 Extract or add shims as necessary and then locate the drivebelt, fit the pulley flange and secure it with the three nuts.

5 If shims have been extracted, keep them for future use by inserting them under the securing nuts on the front flange of the pulley.

6 On cars built after November 1974, the components of the fan assembly have been slightly modified as shown (Fig. 2.7A).

6 Heating and ventilation system - dismantling and reassembly

1 The hot air duct can be removed from the interior of the car after first withdrawing the floor covering.

2 Unscrew and remove the nuts and bolts which secure the air duct to the floor pan, disconnect the front end from the flexible connector and remove the duct (Fig. 2.8 and 2.9).

3 To remove the air blending and distribution unit, which is located under the fascia panel, unscrew the securing nuts and lift it from its location (Fig. 2.10).

4 Once the air blending and distribution unit has been removed, the demister outlets can be extracted from within the rear of the luggage compartment (Fig. 2.11).

5 The main heater control and cover plate can be unbolted from the floor in the rear passenger compartment (Fig. 2.12).

6 Reassembly is a reversal of dismantling but make sure that any foam plastic jointing strips are refitted (or renewed if deformed) and any sealing mastic is renewed where originally found.

7 Periodically inspect the condition and security of the convoluted connecting trunking (Fig. 2.13).

Fig. 2.7. Fan/dynamo drivebelt tension diagram

1 Deflection   2 Pulley flange nuts

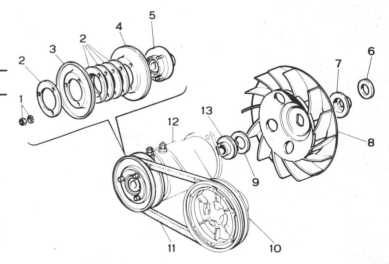

Fig. 2.7A. Fan assembly (Nov. 1974 on)

Keys 1 to 8 as in Fig. 2.6.
9	Washer	12	Dynamo
10	Pulley	13	Hub
11	Belt		

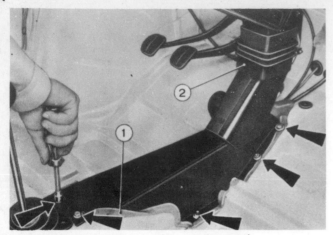

Fig. 2.8. Heater duct attachment nuts (arrowed)

1   *Plastic foam jointing*   2   *Flexible connector*

Fig. 2.11. Demister outlets located within luggage compartment

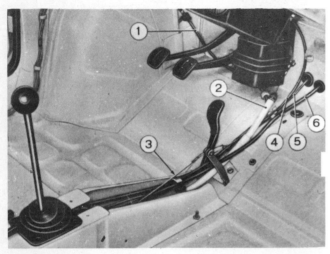

Fig. 2.9. Controls and pipe lines exposed after removal of heater duct

1 *Speedometer cable*	4 *Hand throttle cable*
2 *Clutch operating cable*	5 *Rear brake hydraulic line*
3 *Accelerator cable*	6 *Positive lead from battery*

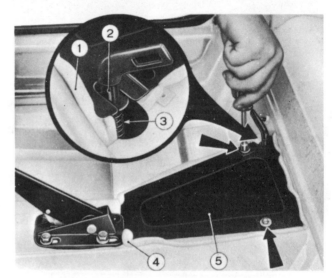

Fig. 2.12. Removing heater duct rear cover

1 *Plastic foam gasket*	4 *Plastic foam gasket*
2 *Air flow control lever*	5 *Rear cover*
3 *Spring*	

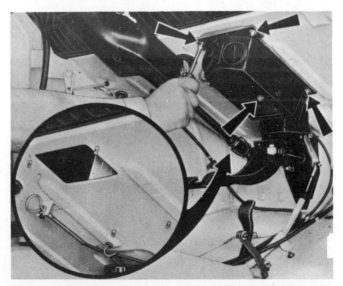

Fig. 2.10. Removing air blending and distribution unit. Inset hand throttle control

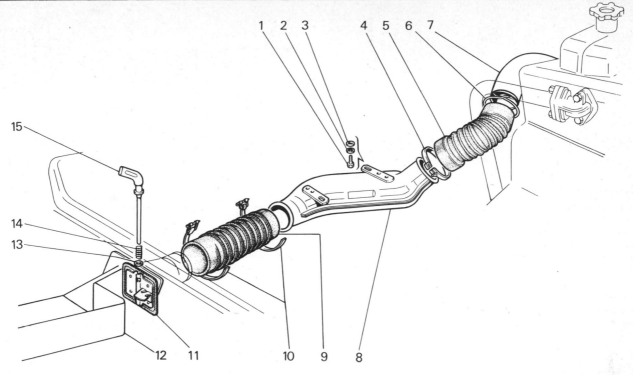

Fig. 2.13. Warm air intake duct components

1	Mounting screw	5	Rear trunking	9	Front trunking	13 Washer
2	Spring washer	6	Clip	10	Plastic hose clip	14 Spring
3	Plain washer	7	Warm air intake nozzle	11	Flap valve	15 Control lever
4	Plastic hose clip	8	Centre duct	12	Floor duct	

7 Fault diagnosis - cooling and heating systems

Symptoms	Reason/s
Engine overheats	Faulty air outlet thermostat. Seized air outlet baffle valve. Lack of engine oil. Broken fan drivebelt. Slipping fan drivebelt. Split or disconnected air inlet trunking to cooling casing.
Engine running cool	Faulty air outlet thermostat. Faulty air outlet baffle valve.
Oil or exhaust fumes evident in car	Blown cylinder head gasket.
Heater ineffective	Disconnected or split connecting trunking. Slipping or broken fan drivebelt. Faulty air outlet thermostat. Seized main heated air inlet valve.

Chapter 3 Carburation; fuel and exhaust systems

Contents

Specifications

System type	Rear mounted fuel tank, mechanically operated fuel pump, single barrel downdraught carburettor
Fuel pump capacity	5.5 Imp. gal/hr (6.6 US gal/hr/25 litres/hr)

Carburettor
Type:

Up to November 1974	Weber 28 IMB 3
After November 1974	Weber 28 IMB 1
Throat diameter	1.102 in (28 mm)
Primary venturi diameter	0.905 in (23 mm)
Auxiliary venturi diameter	0.157 in (4 mm)
Main jet	0.049 in (1.25 mm)
Idling jet	0.018 in (0.45 mm)
Starting jet (F5)	0.035 in (0.90 mm)
Air correction jet:	
Up to 1974	0.085 in (2.15 mm)
After 1974	0.088 in (2.25 mm)
Fuel inlet needle valve	0.049 in (1.25 mm)
Emulsion tube	F8
Idling air orifice	0.079 in (2.00 mm)

Fuel tank capacity	4.6 Imp. gals (5.5 US gals/21 litres)

Torque wrench settings

	lb f ft	Nm
Carburettor mounting nuts	20	28
Fuel pump mounting nuts	20	28
Exhaust manifold elbow bolts	25	35

1 General description

1 The fuel system comprises a rear mounted fuel tank, a mechanically-operated fuel pump, a Weber carburettor and a paper element type air cleaner.
2 Devices to reduce emission of fumes are minimal and consist of the crankcase ventilation system (see Chapter 1, Section 16), a return fuel line from the carburettor and the design of the carburettor which it is anticipated will reduce the CO emission level from the exhaust system when the engine is idling.

2 Air cleaner - servicing

1 At the intervals specified in 'Routine Maintenance', open the lid of the engine compartment and unclip the lid of the air cleaner (photo).

2 Move the lid and connecting pipes to one side and extract the paper type filter element and discard it (Fig. 3.1).
3 Wipe out the air cleaner body and check the condition of the connecting hoses.
4 Install a new filter element making sure that its open end is uppermost.
5 Refit the lid and engage the securing clips.

3 Fuel pump - description, maintenance and testing

1 The fuel pump is of flexible diaphragm type and is located on the left-hand side of the engine crankcase (photo).
2 The pump is actuated by a long pushrod from an eccentric on the camshaft which is located on the opposite side of the engine.
3 At the intervals specified in 'Routine Maintenance', unbolt and remove the cover from the fuel pump.

4   Clean the filter screen in fuel and remove all residual dirt from the pump interior.

5   Check the condition of the sealing edge of the filter and renew it if it is cut or deformed (Fig. 3.2).

6   Reassemble the components but do not overtighten the cover bolt.

7   If, due to lack of fuel at the carburettor, the fuel pump is believed to be at fault, disconnect the fuel feed pipe from the carburettor and place its' open end in a suitable container.

8   Disconnect the LT lead from the negative terminal of the coil to prevent the engine firing and then spin the engine on the starter. A well defined series of spurts of fuel should be ejected into the container. If this happens, reconnect the fuel line and investigate the fuel inlet valve of the carburettor as the cause of the fuel stoppage. If on the other hand, no fuel is ejected from the pipe and some is known to be in the fuel tank, remove the pump for overhaul.

4   Fuel pump - removal and overhaul

1   Disconnect the fuel inlet pipe from the fuel pump and plug the pipe.

2   Disconnect the fuel feed pipe which runs to the carburettor from the fuel pump.

3   Unscrew the two pump flange nuts and withdraw the pump, the insulator and two sealing gaskets (photo).

4   If required, the operating rod can be withdrawn by gripping its end with a pair of pliers (photo).

5   Unbolt and remove the cover.

6   Scribe a line across the edges of the upper and lower body flanges as a guide to reassembly and then unscrew the flange screws and lift the upper body from the lower body.

7   Disconnect the diaphragm/rod assembly from the rocker arm and lift it away.

8   Remove the spacer and springs.

9   Obtain a repair kit which will contain a new flexible diaphragm assembly and the other necessary renewable items.

10 If the inlet and outlet valves are faulty then the complete pump upper body will have to be renewed as the valves cannot be renewed on their own.

11 Reassembly is a reversal of dismantling, but tighten the flange screws evenly in diagonally opposite sequence and only fully tighten them while the rocker arm is held fully depressed towards the pump body.

2.1 Air cleaner components

3.1 Location of fuel pump

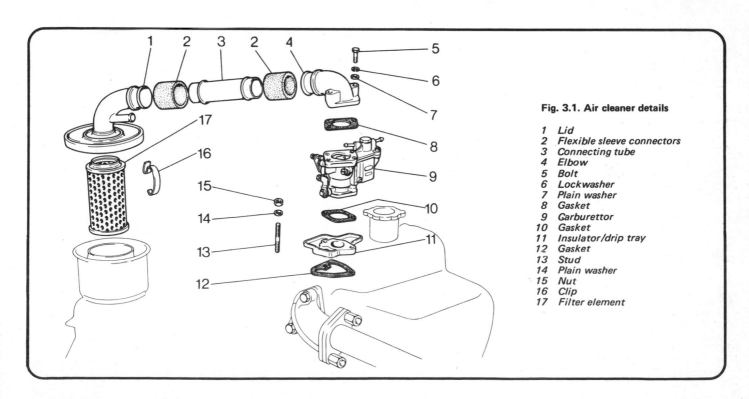

Fig. 3.1. Air cleaner details

1   Lid
2   Flexible sleeve connectors
3   Connecting tube
4   Elbow
5   Bolt
6   Lockwasher
7   Plain washer
8   Gasket
9   Carburettor
10 Gasket
11 Insulator/drip tray
12 Gasket
13 Stud
14 Plain washer
15 Nut
16 Clip
17 Filter element

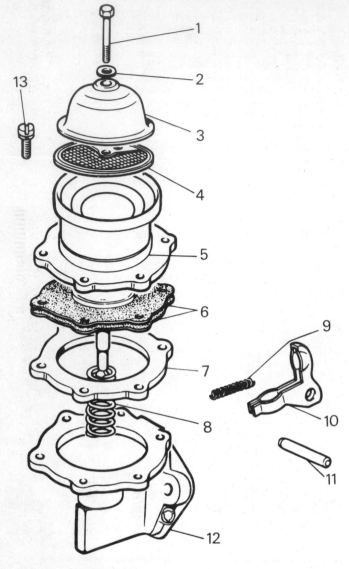

Fig. 3.2. Exploded view of the fuel pump

1	Cover bolt	8	Diaphragm spring
2	Plain washer	9	Rocker arm spring
3	Cover	10	Rocker arm
4	Filter	11	Pivot pin
5	Upper body	12	Lower body
6	Diaphragm	13	Screw
7	Spacer		

5   Fuel pump - refitting

1   To refit the pump, place a gasket (0.027 in /0.7 mm thick) against the crankcase and then install the insulator followed by the second gasket (0.012 in/0.03 mm thick).
2   Insert the pushrod and then turn the crankshaft to the point where the rod is just about to start riding up the eccentric cam of the camshaft. This can be determined by feeling or watching the pushrod just when it starts to move outwards.
3   Now measure the projection of the rod above the outer gasket. This should be between 0.039 and 0.059 in (1 and 1.5 mm) when measured with a feeler blade (Fig. 3.3).
4   If necessary change the inner gasket for one of a different thickness. Gaskets are available in thicknesses of 0.012, 0.027 and 0.047 in (0.3, 0.7 and 1.2 mm).
5   Install the fuel pump, tighten the flange nuts and reconnect the fuel pipes.

6   Fuel tank - removal, repair and installation

1   The fuel tank is located below the left-hand rear seat. It is flange-mounted into the floor pan and projects below the car.
2   To remove the tank, lift out the rear seat, disconnect the leads from the tank sender unit.
3   Disconnect the fuel filler pipe from the tank, also the vent pipe and the fuel feed and return lines.
4   Unbolt and lift the tank from its location.
5   The sealing mastic may have to be cut away before the tank can be released from its mounting flange.
6   If the tank is contaminated with water or sediment, remove the tank sender unit and shake the tank vigorously using two or three changes of paraffin and a final rinse with clean petrol.
7   If there is a leak in the tank, do not be tempted to solder it: either have it professionally repaired, or obtain a new tank.
8   Installation of the tank is a reversal of removal, but check the security of the seal of the tank sender unit and make good the sealing mastic round the tank flange to prevent entry of water.

7   Carburettor and controls - description

1   The carburettor is a single barrel downdraught Weber 28 IMB unit (Fig. 3.4).
2   A manually operated choke is fitted which gives progressive operation as the engine warms up. The choke control lever is located on the floor tunnel to the left of the matching starter control lever (photo).
3   A hand throttle is located under the instrument panel.
4   The accelerator linkage is by means of a cable to a lever which is pivotted on the upper surface of the engine cooling casing and from the lever to the carburettor throttle valve through a short link rod (photo).

8   Carburettor - slow-running adjustment

1   Run the car until the engine is at normal operating temperature.
2   Make sure that the ignition settings are correct.
3   Adjust the throttle speed screw until the engine is running at an acceptable idling speed without being set too slow so that the engine hesitates or 'rocks' violently.
4   Now turn the mixture control screw in, or out, until the engine idles at its smoothest. Now re-adjust the throttle speed screw if the idling speed has increased as a result of adjusting the mixture control screw.

9   Carburettor - removal and refitting

1   Prise off the clips which secure the lid of the air cleaner body.
2   Move the lid and hose assembly to one side and disconnect the flexible connector from the intake elbow on the top of the carburettor.
3   Disconnect the fume extraction hose from the top of the rocker box cover.
4   Disconnect the choke inner cable from the lever on the side of the carburettor and then detach the outer conduit from its support bracket (photo).
5   Release the spring connecting clip and disconnect the throttle operating link rod from the throttle control lever on the carburettor.
6   Disconnect the fuel feed and return pipes from their nozzles on the carburettor (photo).
7   Unscrew and remove the mounting nuts and washers from the flange mounting studs and lift the carburettor from the insulator/drip tray. One of the mounting nuts is very inaccessible and in the absence of a special spanner it is recommended that the rocker cover is removed to provide more clearance (photo).
8   With the carburettor removed, detach the gasket, the drip tray and the second gasket, in that order.
9   Refitting is a reversal of removal but it is recommended that new flange gaskets are used, between the drip tray/insulator and the manifold and the carburettor mounting flange (photo).

4.3 Removing fuel pump

4.4 Withdrawing fuel pump operating rod

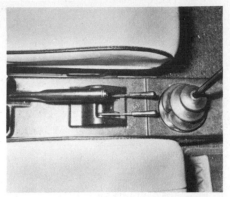

7.2 Choke (left) and starter (right) control levers

7.4a Accelerator control pivot and link

7.4b Accelerator cable conduit bracket

9.4 Choke cable connection to carburettor

9.6 Carburettor showing fuel inlet pipe and return nozzle

9.7 Removing a carburettor flange nut

9.9 Carburettor mounting and insulator/drip tray gaskets

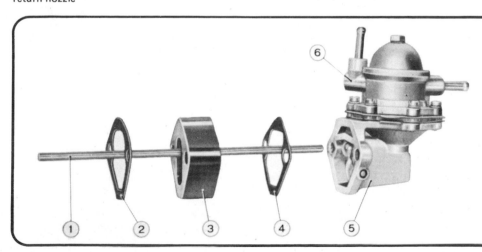

Fig. 3.3. Fuel pump installation details

1 Operating rod
2 Gasket (variable thickness)
3 Insulator
4 Gasket (standard thickness)
5 Fuel pump lower body
6 Fuel pump upper body

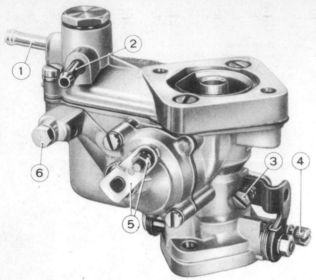

Fig. 3.4. Carburettor details

1   *Fuel return line connection*
2   *Fuel inlet line connection*
3   *Throttle speed screw*
4   *Mixture control screw*
5   *Choke operating lever and inner cable clamp*
6   *Choke cable conduit clamp*

10 Carburettor - maintenance and overhaul

1   The only attention normally required to the carburettor (while installed to the engine) is to apply a few drops of oil to the choke and throttle control pivots and to clean the filter screen at the specified intervals.

2   To clean the filter screen, unscrew the large bolt on the top cover of the carburettor and lift it out together with the filter. Wash the filter gauze in clean fuel and refit it, making sure that the sealing washer under the bolt is in good condition (photo).

3   More extensive dismantling should be carried out in the following way if worn components are to be renewed.

4   With the carburettor removed from the engine, as described in the preceding Section, clean away all external dirt.

5   Unbolt and remove the air cleaner connecting elbow and its gasket.

6   Extract the screws which secure the top cover to the main carburettor body (photo).

7   Lift the top cover complete with float assembly from the carburettor body (photo).

8   The float can be detached from the top cover by extracting the pivot pin. Invert the top cover before removing the float otherwise the fuel inlet needle valve will drop out of its seat (photos).

9   Extract the needle valve and, if necessary, unscrew the needle valve seat using a close-fitting ring spanner.

10   The individual jets can be unscrewed from their seats and are located as shown (Fig. 3.5).

11   The choke cover can be detached after unscrewing the retaining screws (Fig. 3.6).

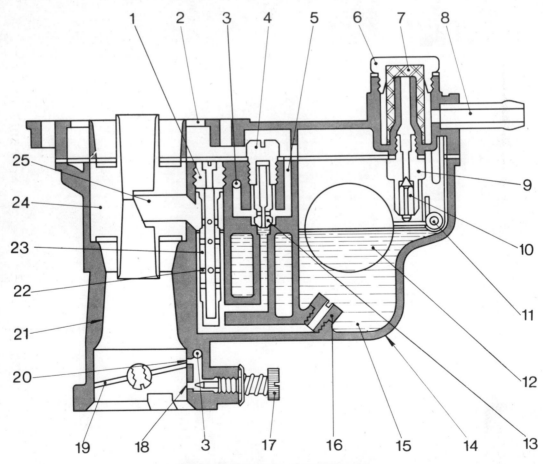

Fig. 3.5. Sectional view of the carburettor

1   *Air correction jet*
2   *Air inlet*
3   *Idle mixture passage*
4   *Idle jet holder*
5   *Idle air orifice*
6   *Filter bolt*
7   *Filter gauge*
8   *Fuel inlet*
9   *Fuel inlet needle valve seat*
10   *Needle valve*
11   *Float pivot pin*
12   *Float*
13   *Idle jet*
14   *Main body*
15   *Fuel bowl*
16   *Main jet*
17   *Idle mixture screw*
18   *Idle orifice*
19   *Throttle butterfly valve plate*
20   *Transfer orifice*
21   *Primary venturi*
22   *Emulsion orifices*
23   *Emulsion tube*
24   *Axuliary venturi*
25   *Nozzle*

12 Any wear occurring in the throttle valve spindle should be rectified by renewing the carburettor complete, as it is not possible to restore the spindle bearing surfaces which are drilled directly in the carburettor body.

13 With the carburettor dismantled, clean out the float chamber. Clean all the jets by blowing through them with air from a tyre pump. Never probe them with wire or their calibration will be upset. It is worthwhile checking the jet sizes with those given in the Specifications in case a previous owner has substituted any of incorrect size.

14 Obtain a repair kit which will contain all the necessary gaskets and other items which must be renewed.

15 Reassemble by installing the jets. Tighten them securely using close fitting screwdriver blades of correct width and thickness to suit the slots in the jets.

16 Make sure that the washer is included under the fuel inlet seat before tightening it firmly. Do not overtighten it, but make sure that it grips the washer and 'bites' otherwise fuel will bypass the needle valve and cause flooding from the fuel bowl.

17 Once the float and needle valve have been reassembled, check the float level. To do this, place a new gasket on the top cover mating flange and then hold the top cover vertically so that the weight of the float and arm rests on the needle valve. The distance 'A' between the lowest point of the float and the surface of the gasket should be 0.315 in (8 mm) (Fig. 3.7).

18 Now move the float gently outward until it stops and again measure the distance 'B' which should be 0.630 in (16 mm) thus providing a float travel of 0.315 in (8 mm). After November 1974, the distance 'A' has been reduced to 0.275 in (7 mm).

19 Any adjustment required to alter the float setting should be carried out by bending the tongue or lug on the float arm.

20 Before installing the top cover, pour a little fuel into the float chamber. This will make starting easier once the carburettor is refitted to the engine, but remember to keep the carburettor in an upright attitude until it is installed.

21 Refit the remaining components by reversing the dismantling operations.

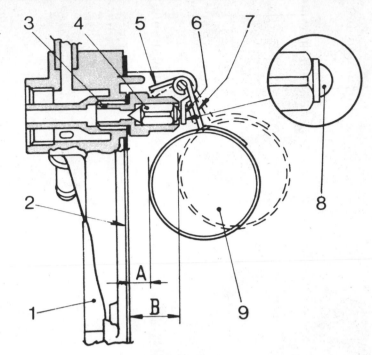

Fig. 3.7. Float adjustment diagram

1	Carburettor top cover	6	Float arm tongue
2	Cover gasket	7	Float arm
3	Needle valve seat	8	Needle valve
4	Needle valve	9	Float
5	Float arm lug		

For values of A and B - see text.

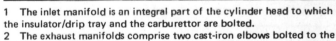

11 Manifolds and exhaust system - general

1 The inlet manifold is an integral part of the cylinder head to which the insulator/drip tray and the carburettor are bolted.

2 The exhaust manifolds comprise two cast-iron elbows bolted to the cylinder head (photo).

3 The exhaust system is an integral assembly comprising downpipes, silencer and tailpipe and is renewable as such (photo).

4 When fitting the exhaust flanges to the cylinder head, note the thin washers used to seal the joints.

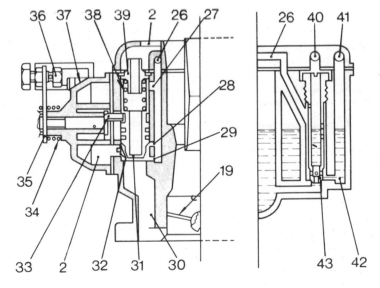

Fig. 3.6. Sectional views of choke mechanism

2	Air inlet	35	Choke control lever
19	Throttle valve plate	36	Cable clamp screw
26	Mixture passage	37	Cable conduit clamp
27	Mixture weakening air passage	38	Valve spring
28	Mixture orifices	39	Spring retainer and guide
29	Mixture orifices	40	Starter jet emulsion air orifice
30	Mixture passage	41	Reserve well emulsion air orifice
31	Choke valve		
32	Air orifices	42	Reserve well
33	Rocker	43	Starter jet
34	Lever return spring		

10.2 Extracting carburettor fuel filter

10.6 Removing a top cover screw from carburettor

10.7 Removing carburettor top cover

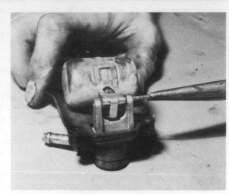

10.8a Extracting float pivot

10.8b Removing carburettor float to expose fuel inlet valve

11.2 Exhaust manifold and gasket (one side)

11.3 The exhaust system

12 Fault diagnosis - carburation; fuel and exhaust systems

Symptom	Reason/s
Excessive fuel consumption	Air filter choked. Leakage from pump, carburettor or fuel lines or fuel tank. Float chamber flooding. Distributor capacitor faulty. Distributor weights faulty. Mixture too rich. Contact breaker gap too wide. Incorrect valve clearances. Incorrect spark plug gaps. Tyres under inflated. Dragging brakes.
Fuel starvation or mixture weakness	Clogged fuel filter in pump or carburettor. Float chamber needle valve clogged. Faulty fuel pump valves. Fuel pump diaphragm split. Fuel pipe unions loose. Fuel pump cover leaking. Inlet manifold gasket or carburettor flange gasket leaking. Incorrect adjustment of carburettor.

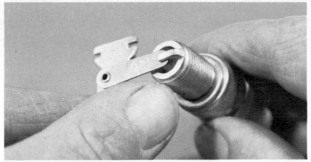

Measuring plug gap. A feeler gauge of the correct size (see ignition system specifications) should have a slight 'drag' when slid between the electrodes. Adjust gap if necessary

Adjusting plug gap. The plug gap is adjusted by bending the earth electrode inwards, or outwards, as necessary until the correct clearance is obtained. Note the use of the correct tool

Normal. Grey-brown deposits lightly coated core nose. Gap increasing by around 0.001 in (0.025 mm) per 1000 miles (1600 km). Plugs ideally suited to engine and engine in good condition

Carbon fouling. Dry, black, sooty deposits. Will cause weak spark and eventually misfire. Fault: over-rich fuel mixture. Check: carburettor mixture settings, float level and jet sizes; choke operation and cleanliness of air filter. Plugs can be re-used after cleaning

Oil fouling. Wet, oily deposits. Will cause weak spark and eventually misfire. Fault: worn bores/piston rings or valve guides; sometimes occurs (temporarily) during running-in period. Plugs can be re-used after thorough cleaning

Overheating. Electrodes have glazed appearance, core nose very white - few deposits. Fault: plug overheating. Check: plug value, ignition timing, fuel octane rating (too low) and fuel mixture (too weak). Discard plugs and cure fault immediately

Electrode damage. Electrodes burned away; core nose has burned, glazed appearance. Fault: initial pre-ignition. Check: as for 'Overheating' but may be more severe. Discard plugs and remedy fault before piston or valve damage occurs

Split core nose (may appear initially as a crack). Damage is self-evident, but cracks will only show after cleaning. Fault: pre-ignition or wrong gap-setting technique. Check: ignition timing, cooling system, fuel octane rating (too low) and fuel mixture (too weak). Discard plugs, rectify fault immediately

Chapter 4 Ignition system

Contents

Specifications

System type ... ...   12V negative earth, battery, coil and distributor

Distributor

Contact breaker points gap	0.018 to 0.021 in (0.47 to 0.53 mm)
Firing order	1 - 2
Rotation	Anticlockwise
Static advance	10° BTDC
Maximum centrifugal advance	18° BTDC

Condenser

Capacity at between 50 and 1000 Hz	0.25 microformed

Coil

	Marelli BE 200 B	Martinetti G 52 S
Type	Marelli BE 200 B	Martinetti G 52 S
Primary winding resistance (at 68°F - 20°C)	3.1 to 3.4 ohms	3.0 to 3.3 ohms
Secondary winding resistance (at 68°F - 20°C)	6750 to 8250 ohms	6500 to 8000 ohms

Spark plugs

	Marelli CW 8 NP	Champion L 81 Y
Type	Marelli CW 8 NP	Champion L 81 Y
Size	14 mm	14 mm
Gap	0.023 to 0.027 in (0.6 to 0.7 mm)	

Torque wrench settings

	lb f ft	Nm
Distributor clamp bolt	15	21
Spark plugs	22	30

1 General description

1 The ignition system is conventional, having a battery, coil and distributor with mechanical contact breaker.

2 When the ignition is switched on a current flows from the battery live terminal to the ignition switch through the coil primary winding to the moving contact breaker inside the distributor cap and to earth when the contact breaker points are in the closed position. During this period of points closure, the current flows through the primary windings of the coil and magnetises the laminated iron core which in turn creates a magnetic field through the coil primary and secondary windings.

3 Each time the points open due to the rotation of the distributor cam, the current flow through the primary winding of the coil is interrupted. This causes the induction of a very high voltage (25,000 volts) in the coil secondary winding. This HT (high tension) current is distributed to the spark plugs in correct firing order sequence by the rotor arm and by means of the cap brush and HT leads.

4 A condenser is fitted to the distributor and connected between the moving contact breaker and earth to prevent excessive arcing and pitting of the contact breaker points.

5 The actual point of ignition of the fuel/air mixture which occurs a few degrees before TDC is determined by correct static setting of the ignition timing as described in Section 8. The ignition is advanced to meet varying operating conditions by the centrifugal counterweights fitted in the base of the distributor.

2 Contact breaker - adjustment

1 Open the lid of the engine compartment and unclip and remove the cap from the distributor.

2 Pull off the rotor arm.

3 Turn the crankshaft until the heel of the contact breaker arm is on one of the high points of the cam of the distributor shaft.

4 Using a feeler blade, check that the gap is as specified in the Specifications Section. If the gap is incorrect, loosen the screw which

secures the fixed contact breaker arm to the baseplate, insert a screwdriver blade in the slot provided in the arm and turn the blade, so moving the contact breaker arm as necessary to adjust the gap. Tighten the securing screw (photo).

5   If the faces of the contact points are severely burned or a 'pip' has built up on one of them, then any checking of the gap with a feeler blade will produce a false reading. The points, if in this condition, must be removed and either renovated or renewed, as described in the next Section.

3   Contact breaker points - removal and refitting

1   Remove the distributor cap and rotor arm, as described in the preceding Section.
2   Release both the locknuts on the LT terminal on the side of the distributor body and unscrew them as far as possible without actually removing them from the terminal stud.
3   Push the terminal stud inwards and release the spring arm of the movable contact arm.
4   Unscrew and remove the screw which secures the fixed contact arm to the distributor baseplate and then withdraw the contact breaker assembly complete.
5   If the points are badly pitted or a 'pip' has built up on one of them, draw a strip of abrasive paper through them until they are clean and square. It is possible to dismantle the contact breaker by extracting the circlip at the top of the pivot post if more extensive dressing of the points is to be carried out on an oilstone, but this is not recommended and if the points are in such a poor condition as this then they should be renewed.
6   Install the new points by reversing the removal operations and set the gap, as described in the preceding Section.
7   Whenever new points are installed as at the intervals specified in 'Routine Maintenance' apply two or three drops of engine oil to the felt pad on the top of the distributor shaft.

4   Condenser (capacitor) - removal, testing and refitting

1   The condenser ensures that with the contact breaker points open, the sparking between them is not excessive, as this would cause severe pitting. The condenser is fitted in parallel and its failure will automatically cause failure of the ignition system as the points will be prevented from interrupting the low tension circuit.
2   Testing for an unserviceable condenser may be effected by switching on the ignition and separating the contact points by hand. If this action is accompanied by a blue flash then condenser failure is indicated. Difficult starting, missing of the engine after several miles running or badly pitted points are other indications of a faulty condenser.
3   The surest test is by substitution of a new unit.
4   To remove the condenser, unscrew its retaining screw and detach its lead from the LT terminal on the distributor body. Refitting is a reversal of removal.

5   Distributor - removal

1   Although the marking of the distributor described in this Section is not essential if the installation procedure, described in Section 7, is carefully followed, it will save time and avoid confusion if the following operations are adhered to.
2   Open the lid of the engine compartment, unclip the lid from the distributor and move it to one side.
3   Unscrew the LT terminal nut and pull off the LT lead. Temporarily refit the terminal nut.
4   Unscrew the spark plug nearest the back of the car and hold the thumb over the plug hole. Turn the crankshaft until compression can be felt being generated in No. 1 cylinder as the piston rises.
5   Continue to turn the crankshaft until the ignition timing mark on the cover of the centrifugal oil filter is opposite the static advance mark on the timing cover (Fig. 4.1). From 1974 the timing mark on the filter cover takes the form of a notch in the pulley flange nearest the engine.
6   Dot punch the rim of the distributor body at a point in alignment

with the contact end of the rotor arm.
7   Dot punch the position of the distributor body lower flange in relation to the engine crankcase.
8   Unscrew and remove the clamp nut and withdraw the distributor from the engine (photo).

2.4 Checking contact breaker points gap

5.8 Distributor clamp plate and nut

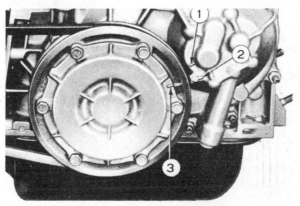

Fig. 4.1. Ignition timing marks

1   Static advance (10°) mark   2   TDC mark
3   Filter cover alignment work

6 Distributor - overhaul

1   It is recommended that general wear in the distributor internal components is rectified by renewal of the unit.
2   Access to the counterweights and springs can be obtained after extracting the baseplate screws and removing the baseplate.
3   The cam assembly can be removed after the felt pad has been extracted from the top of the shaft and the screw withdrawn. Always mark which way round the cam is fitted to the shaft.
4   The driven gear at the base of the shaft is secured by a pin.
5   Examine the carbon brush in the distributor cap. If it has worn away, renew it.
6   If the contact on the end of the rotor arm is severely burned, renew the arm.

7 Distributor - installation

1   If the original distributor is being refitted, make sure that the static advance ignition marks are in alignment by turning the crankshaft, as described in Section 5.
2   The distributor rotates in an anticlockwise direction and as it is installed, the meshing of the driven gear at the base of the distributor shaft with the drive gear on the camshaft will cause the rotor arm to turn. Therefore set the contact end of the rotor arm about 30° in a clockwise direction from the alignment mark made on the distributor body rim while the distributor is held over its recess in the crankcase in approximately the correct position for installation (photo).
3   Install the distributor and the rotor will turn and take up a position in correct alignment with the punch mark on the rim (photo).
4   Check that the distributor body to crankcase marks are also in alignment and then that the contact points are just about to open.
5   Secure the distributor by installing the clamp and its securing nut.
6   If the distributor was removed without making alignment marks or a new distributor is being installed, make a mark on the rim of the distributor body which is in line with No 1 (rearmost cylinder) HT lead contact in the distributor cap.
7   Turn the rotor arm about 30° in a clockwise direction from this mark on the rim and then hold the distributor over its recess in the crankcase so that the condenser is almost directly over the hole into which the engine oil dipstick fits (Fig. 4.2).
8   Push the distributor into place when the rotor arm will turn and align with the rim mark.
9   Turn the distributor body in either direction until the contact breaker points are just about to open and then fit the clamp plate and nut.
10 Reconnect the cap and HT leads, reconnect the LT lead.
11 Check the ignition timing, as described in Section 8, using a stroboscope.

8 Ignition timing - adjustment

1   On most cars, two timing marks are located on the timing cover. The arrow indicates TDC while the raised line indicates the advance mark (10° BTDC).
2   A short raised line is located on the cover of the centrifugal oil filter.
3   On some cars, the advance mark on the timing cover is not incorporated but a line can be made by painting or scribing one through the centres of the two raised bosses on the timing cover.
4   Set the initial (static) advance by turning the crankshaft until the mark on the oil filter cover is opposite to the advance mark on the timing cover with No 1 piston on its compression stroke. The crankshaft can be turned by removing the spark plugs and gripping the oil filter/pulley with the hands. Alternatively, place the car in top gear and push it forward.
5   The fact that No 1 piston (nearest rear of car) is on its compression stroke can be ascertained in one of two ways. Either remove a spark plug and with the finger over the hole, feel the compression being generated, or remove the rocker cover and watch the positions of the rocker arms. When the rocker arms of No. 2 cylinder are 'in balance' (any slight movement of the crankshaft in either direction will cause one or other of the rocker arms to move) then the two valves of No 1 cylinder will be closed and the piston near the top of its compression stroke.

6   With the timing marks correctly set, release the distributor clamp plate nut and turn the distributor until the contact points are just about to open.
7   Tighten the clamp plate nut.
8   It is recommended that the ignition timing is now checked with a stroboscope after the engine has been run to normal operating temperature.
9   To do this, first paint the mark on the oil filter cover and the 'ADVANCE' mark on the timing cover with quick drying white paint.
10 Connect the stroboscope in accordance with the manufacturer's instructions (usually between No 1 spark plug and the end of its HT lead).
11 Start the engine and let it idle at its specified slow-running speed.
12 Project the light from the stroboscope onto the timing marks. The pulley mark will appear to be stationary and in alignment with the 'ADVANCE' mark on the timing cover. If it is not in alignment, release the distributor clamp screw and turn the distributor until the marks do coincide. Retighten the clamp screw.
13 A useful check on the operation of the centrifugal advance mechanism can now be made by revving the engine and watching the movement of the timing marks (still under the light from the stroboscope). The mark on the pulley should move out of alignment with the timing cover pointer and the amount of misalignment will increase in proportion to the increase in engine speed. This proves correct operation of the centrifugal advance mechanism. The timing marks should resume their alignment when the engine speed returns to idling. No vacuum advance is fitted to this distributor.
14 Switch off the engine, remove the stroboscope and re-make the original connections.

9 Coil - polarity and testing

1   High tension current should be negative at the spark plug terminals. If the HT current is positive at the spark plug terminals then the LT leads to the coil primary terminals have been incorrectly connected. A wrong connection can cause as much as 60% loss of spark efficiency and can cause rough idling and misfiring at speed (photo).
2   With a negative earth electrical system, the LT lead from the distributor connects with the negative (primary) terminal on the coil.
3   The simplest way to test a coil is by substitution. If an ohmmeter is available, use it to carry out the following checks, but first apply a 12 volt current to the coil to bring it to normal operating temperature.
4   Check the primary resistance between the coil (+) and (–) terminals which should be as shown in the Specifications Section.
5   Check the secondary resistance (secondary to primary terminals) this should be as shown in the Specifications Section.
6   Insulation breakdown can only be satisfactorily tested using a megohmmeter between the coil casing and the primary terminals. The resistance should be in excess of 50 megohms.

10 Spark plugs and HT leads - general

1   The correct functioning of the spark plugs is vital for the correct running and efficiency of the engine. The plugs fitted as standard are listed in the Specification page.
2   At the specified intervals, the plugs should be removed, examined, cleaned and, if worn excessively, renewed. The condition of the spark plug will also tell much about the overall condition of the engine.
3   If the insulator nose of the spark plug is clean and white, with no deposits, this is indicative of a weak mixture, or too hot a plug.
4   If the top and insulator nose is covered with hard black looking deposits, this is indicative of a weak mixture, or too hot a plug. plug be black and oily, then it is likely that the engine is fairly worn, as well as the mixture being too rich.
5   If the insulator nose is covered with light tan to greyish brown deposits, then the mixture is correct and it is likely that the engine is in good condition.
6   If there are any traces of long brown tapering stains on the outside of the white portion of the plug, then the plug will have to be renewed, as this shows that there is a faulty joint between the plug body and the insulator, and compression is being allowed to leak away.
7   Plugs should be cleaned by a sand blasting machine, which will free them from carbon more thoroughly than cleaning by hand. The

7.2 Distributor ready for installation

7.3 Distributor installed

9.1 The ignition coil

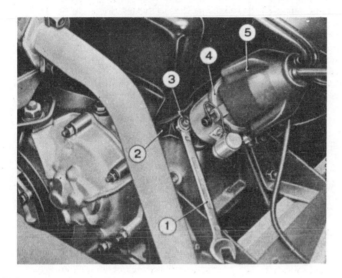

Fig. 4.2. Distributor installation

1 Spanner	4 Distributor
2 Distributor clamp	5 Moisture protection cover
3 Clamp nut	

machine will also test the condition of the plugs under compression. Any plug that fails to spark at the recommended pressure should be renewed.

8 The spark plug gap is of considerable importance, as, if it is too large or too small the size of the spark and its efficiency will be seriously impaired. The spark plug gap should be set to between 0.023 to 0.027 in (0.6 to 0.7 mm) for the best results.

9 To set it, measure the gap with a feeler gauge, and then bend open, or close the outer plug electrode until the correct gap is achieved. The centre electrode should never be bent as this may crack the insulation and cause plug failure.

10 The HT leads are of copper cored cable with separate interference suppressor which are screwed onto the spark plugs.

11 Occasionally wipe the cables clean with a petrol soaked rag.

12 Always check that the cables are connected between the distributor cap and the spark plugs correctly (see Fig. 4.4).

11 Ignition system - fault diagnosis

Failures of the ignition system will either be due to faults in the HT or LT circuits. Initial checks should be made by observing the security of spark plug terminals, switch terminals, coil and battery connection. More detailed investigation and the explanation and remedial action in respect of symptoms of ignition malfunction are described in the following sub-sections.

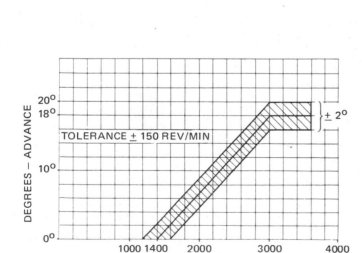

Fig. 4.3. Centrifugal advance diagram

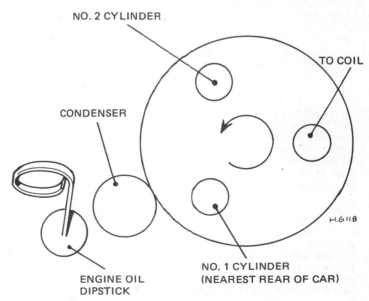

Fig. 4.4. Distributor HT lead connection diagram

Engine fails to start

1   If the engine fails to start and the car was running normally when it was used last, first check there is fuel in the tank. If the engine turns over normally on the starter motor and the battery is evidently well charged, then the fault may be in either the high or low tension circuits. First check the HT circuit. **Note:** If the battery is known to be fully charged; the ignition light comes on, and the starter motor fails to turn the engine check the tightness of the leads on the battery terminals and also the security of the earth lead to its connection to the body. It is quite common for the leads to have worked loose, even if they look and feel secure. If one of the battery terminal posts gets very hot when trying to work the starter motor this is a sure indication of a faulty connection to that terminal.

2   One of the commonest reasons for bad starting is wet or damp spark plug leads and distributor. Remove the distributor cap. If condensation is visible internally, dry the cap with a rag and also wipe over the leads. Replace the cap.

3   If the engine still fails to start, check that current is reaching the plugs, by disconnecting each plug lead in turn at the spark plug end, and hold the end of the cable about 3/16 in (4.7 mm) away from the cylinder block. Spin the engine on the starter motor.

4   Sparking between the end of the cable and block should be fairly strong with a regular blue spark. (Hold the lead with rubber to avoid electric shocks). If current is reaching the plugs, then remove them and clean and regap them. The engine should now start.

5   If there is no spark at the plug leads take off the HT lead from the centre of the distributor cap and hold it to the block as before. Spin the engine on the starter once more. A rapid succession of blue sparks between the end of the lead and the block indicate that the coil is in order and that the distributor cap is cracked, the rotor arm faulty, or the carbon brush in the top of the distributor cap is not making good contact with the spring on the rotor arm. Possibly the points are in bad condition. Clean and reset them as described in this Chapter.

6   If there are no sparks from the end of the lead from the coil, check the connections at the coil end of the lead. If it is in order start checking the low tension circuit.

7   Use a 12v voltmeter or a 12v bulb and two lengths of wire. With the ignition switch on and the points open test between the low tension wire to the coil (it is marked +) and earth. No reading indicates a break in the supply from the ignition switch. Check the connections at the switch to see if any are loose. Refit them and the engine should run. A reading shows a faulty coil or condenser, or broken lead between the coil and the distributor.

8   Take the condenser wire off the points assembly and with the points open, test between the moving point and earth. If there now is a reading, then the fault is in the condenser. Fit a new one and the fault is cleared.

9   With no reading from the moving contact breaker point to earth, take a reading between earth and the (—) terminal of the coil. A reading

here shows a broken wire which will need to be renewed between the coil and distributor. No reading confirms that the coil has failed and must be renewed, after which the engine will run once more. Remember to refit the condenser wire to the points assembly. For these tests it is sufficient to separate the points with a piece of dry paper while testing with the points open.

Engine misfires

10   If the engine misfires regularly run it at a fast idling speed. Pull off each of the plug caps in turn and listen to the note of the engine. Hold the plug cap in a dry cloth or with a rubber glove as additional protection against shock from the HT supply.

11   No difference in engine running will be noticed when the lead from the defective circuit is removed. Removing the lead from the good cylinder will accentuate the misfire.

12   Remove the plug lead from the end of the defective plug and hold it about 3/16 in (5 mm) away from the block. Restart the engine. If the sparking is fairly strong and regular the fault must lie in the spark plug.

13   The plug may be loose, the insulation may be cracked, or the points may have burnt away giving too wide a gap for the spark to jump. Worse still, one of the points may have broken off. Either renew the plug, or clean it, reset the gap, and then test it.

14   If there is no spark at the end of the plug lead, or if it is weak and intermittent, check the ignition lead from the distributor to the plug. If the insulation is cracked or perished, renew the lead. Check the connection at the distributor cap.

15   If there is still no spark, examine the distributor cap carefully for tracking. This can be recognised by a very thin black line running between the two contacts, or between a contact and some other part of the distributor. These lines are paths which now conduct electricity across the cap thus letting it run to earth. The only answer is a new distributor cap.

16   Apart from the ignition timing being incorrect, other causes of misfiring have already been dealt with under the Section dealing with the failure of the engine to start. To recap - these are that:

a)   The coil may be faulty giving an intermittent misfire.
b)   There may be a damaged wire or loose connection in the low tension circuit.
c)   The condenser may be short circuiting.
d)   There may be a mechanical fault in the distributor (broken driving spindle or contact breaker spring).

17   If the ignition timing is too far retarded, it should be noted that the engine will tend to overheat, and there will be a quite noticeable drop in power. If the engine is overheating and the power is down, and the ignition timing is correct, then the carburettor should be checked, as it is likely that this is where the fault lies.

Chapter 5 Clutch

Contents

Specifications

Type	Single dry plate, diaphragm spring with cable actuation	
Drive plate diameter	6.1 in (155 mm)	
Pedal free-movement	1.1 in (28 mm)	

Torque wrench settings	lb f ft	Nm
Release fork lockbolt	18	25
Pressure plate cover bolts to flywheel	12	16
Bellhousing bolts to engine	18	25

1 General description

1 The clutch is of single dry plate, diaphragm spring type.
2 Clutch actuation is by cable from a pendant type foot pedal.

2 Clutch - adjustment

1 The free-movement at the clutch pedal should be maintained at just over 1 in (28 mm).
2 Measure the free-movement carefully by holding a rule against the side of the clutch pedal and depressing the pedal with the fingers until resistance can be felt. The distance over which the pedal has moved from the fully released position to the point where resistance is felt is the free-movement.
3 The free-movement can be increased, or decreased, by releasing the locknut on the threaded part at the end of the clutch cable within the engine compartment and turning the adjuster nut in the appropriate direction (Fig. 5.1).
4 Re-check the free-movement, and then tighten the locknut without altering the position of the adjuster nut.
5 Always keep the threaded end of the clutch cable well smeared with grease to prevent corrosion of the threads.

3 Clutch cable - renewal

1 Disconnect the threaded end of the clutch cable from the release lever on the clutch bellhousing by unscrewing the adjuster nut and locknut (Fig. 5.2).
2 Disconnect the outer cable bracket adjacent to the release lever.

3 Disconnect the opposite end of the cable from the clutch pedal by extracting the split pin and the cotter pin.
4 Working within the car, remove the heater duct from the floorpan, as described in Chapter 2, Section 6.
5 The clutch cable is now accessible and can be withdrawn through its sealing grommets and a new one installed.
6 Adjust the cable to provide the correct pedal free-movement, as described in the preceding Section.

Fig. 5.1. Clutch cable adjusting nuts

1	Release lever	3 Return spring
2	Adjusting nuts	4 Cable

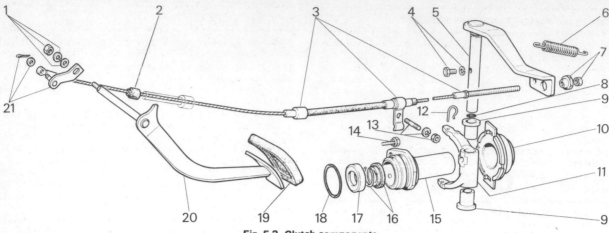

Fig. 5.2. Clutch components

1	Pivot nut and washers	7	Adjuster nut and locknut	12	Spring clip	17	Bush
2	Boot	8	Seal	13	Bracket stud and nut	18	Seal
3	Cable assembly	9	Bush	14	Bearing hub securing bolt	19	Pedal rubber
4	Lockbolt	10	Release bearing	15	Release bearing mounting hub	20	Clutch pedal
5	Release lever/shaft	11	Fork	16	Oil seal	21	Relay lever assembly
6	Return spring						

4 Clutch pedal - removal and installation

1 The pendant type clutch pedal is supported by a pivot bolt attached to a bracket assembly under the fascia panel.
2 To remove the pedal, disconnect the clutch cable from the lever on the end of the pedal pivot bolt.
3 Unscrew the nut which secures the lever to the flats on the end of the pivot bolt and remove the lever and washers. Withdraw the pedal/pivot bolt assembly.
4 Install the pedal by reversing the removal operations, but apply grease to the pivot bolt.
5 There is no provision for adjusting the pedal height and a fixed backstop is incorporated in the pedal arm but adjust the free-movement after installation, as described in Section 2.

5 Clutch - removal

1 Access to the clutch is attained by removing the gearbox as described in Chapter 6, Section 3.
2 Should the engine have to be removed for major overhaul, always take the opportunity to check the clutch components.
3 With the gearbox removed, unbolt and remove the clutch pressure plate from the flywheel. Unscrew the bolts evenly and in diagonally opposite sequence.
4 Withdraw the pressure plate/cover assembly and catch the driven plate which will be released.

6 Clutch - inspection and renovation

1 Examine the clutch disc friction linings for wear and loose rivets and the disc for rim distortion, cracks, and worn splines. The surfaces of the friction linings may be highly glazed, but as long as the clutch material pattern can be clearly seen this is satisfactory. Compare the amount of lining wear with a new clutch disc at the stores in your local garage, and if the linings are more than three quarters worn renew the disc (Fig. 5.3).
2 It is always best to renew the clutch driven plate as an assembly to preclude further trouble but if it is wished to merely renew the linings, the rivets should be drilled out and not knocked out with a punch. The manufacturers do not advise that only the linings are renewed and personal experience dictates that it is far more satisfactory to renew the driven plate complete than to try to economise by only fitting new friction linings.
3 Check the machined faces of the flywheel and the pressure plate. If either are grooved they should be renewed.

4 If the pressure plate is cracked or split it is essential that an exchange unit is fitted, also if the pressure of the diaphragm spring is suspect. It is not practical to dismantle the pressure plate assembly as it will have been accurately set up and balanced to very fine limits.
5 If a new clutch disc is being fitted, it is a false economy not to renew the release bearing at the same time. This will preclude having to replace it at a later date when wear on the clutch linings is still very small.
6 Check the release bearing for smoothness of operation. There should be no harshness and no slackness in it. It should spin reasonably freely bearing in mind it has been pre-packed with grease.

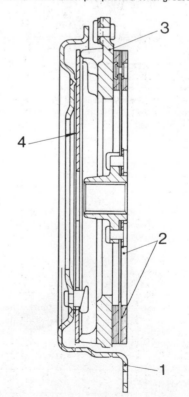

Fig. 5.3. Sectional view of clutch assembly

1	Clutch cover	3	Pressure plate
2	Driven plate	4	Diaphragm spring

7 Clutch release bearing and mechanism - overhaul

1   From within the clutch bellhousing, extract the two small spring clips which secure the release bearing to the release fork (photo).

2   Withdraw the release bearing from the hub on which it slides.

3   If there is any evidence of oil leakage within the clutch bellhousing, this is probably coming from a defective oil seal in the release bearing hub.

4   The bush and oil seal are both renewable and can be drifted from the release bearing hub using a suitable drift after the hub has been unbolted (photo).

5   Wear in the release fork shaft bushes can be rectified if the release fork/shaft assembly is removed. To do this, turn the fork right-over to expose the lockbolt, unscrew the bolt and withdraw the shaft and fork (photo).

6   Extract the old bushes and press in new ones.

7   Reassembly is a reversal of dismantling, but apply grease to the release shaft bushes and to the outer surface of the release bearing mounting hub, also to the contact area between release fork and bearing.

8   It is recommended that new spring clips are used to retain the release bearing to the fork.

9   Renew the spigot bush in the centre of the flywheel mounting flange of the crankshaft if it is worn as described in Chapter 1, Sec 18.

8 Clutch - installation

1   Before the driven plate and pressure plate assembly can be refitted to the flywheel, a centralising guide tool must be obtained or made up. This may be either an old input shaft from a dismantled gearbox or a stepped mandrel.

2   Locate the driven plate against the face of the flywheel ensuring that its flatter side is against the flywheel.

3   Offer up the pressure plate assembly to the flywheel aligning the marks made prior to dismantling and insert the retaining bolts finger-tight only. Where a new pressure plate assembly is being fitted, locate it to the flywheel in a similar relative position to the original by reference to the index marking and dowel positions.

4   Insert the guide tool through the splined hub of the driven plate so that the end of the tool locates in the flywheel spigot bush. This action of the guide tool will centralise the driven plate by causing it to move in a sideways direction (photo).

5   Insert and remove the guide tool two or three times to ensure that the driven plate is fully centralised and then tighten the pressure plate securing bolts a turn at a time and in a diametrically opposite sequence to the specified torque in order to prevent distortion of the pressure plate cover.

6   Refit the gearbox, after reference to Chapter 6, and then adjust the clutch pedal free-movement.

7.1 Clutch release bearing installed

7.4 Clutch release bearing hub

7.5 Clutch release fork showing lockbolt

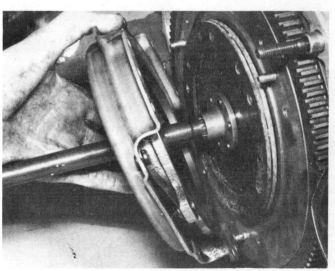

8.4 Assembling and centralising the clutch driven plate

9 Fault diagnosis - clutch

Symptoms	Reason/s
Judder when taking up drive	Loose engine or gearbox mountings. Badly worn friction surfaces or contaminated with oil. Worn splines on gearbox input shaft or driven plate hub. Worn input shaft spigot bush in flywheel.
Clutch spin (failure to disengage) so that gears cannot be meshed	Incorrect release bearing to diaphragm spring due to rust. May occur after vehicle standing idle for long period. Damaged or misaligned pressure plate assembly. Incorrect pedal free-movement.
Clutch slip (increase in engine speed does not result in increase in vehicle road speed - particularly on gradients)	Incorrect release bearing to diaphragm spring finger clearance caused by wrong pedal free-movement. Friction surfaces worn out or oil contaminated.
Noise evident on depressing clutch pedal	Dry, worn or damaged release bearing. Insufficient pedal free-travel. Weak or broken pedal return spring. Weak or broken clutch release lever return spring. Excessive play between driven plate hub splines and input shaft splines.
Noise evident as clutch pedal released	Distorted driven plate. Insufficient pedal free-travel. Weak or broken clutch pedal return spring. Weak or broken release lever return spring. Distorted or worn input shaft. Release bearing loose on retainer hub.

Chapter 6 Gearbox and final drive

Contents

Specifications

Gearbox type	Four forward speeds and reverse. Synchromesh on upper three ratios. Final drive incorporated in gearcase.

Ratios

1st	3.250 : 1
2nd	2.067 : 1
3rd	1.300 : 1
4th	0.872 : 1
Reverse	4.024 : 1

Final drive	4.875 : 1 (8/39)

Oil capacity	2 Imp. pts (2.3 US pts/1.1 litres)

Torque wrench settings	lb f ft	Nm
Gearcase to bellhousing bolt	25	35
Bellhousing to engine bolt	18	25
Pinion shaft and countershaft castillated nuts	36	50
Crownwheel bolts	33	46

1 General description

1   The gearbox is of four forward speed type with reverse gear. Synchromesh is incorporated on the upper three ratios.
2   The gearshift lever is floor-mounted.
3   The differential/final drive assembly is incorporated in the gear casing.
4   Power is transmitted to the rear roadwheels through open drive-shafts (see Chapter 7) (Fig. 6.1).
5   The engine, gearbox and final drive are mounted as one assembly at the rear of the car but the gearbox/final drive can be removed independently leaving the engine in position in the car.
Note: Throughout the text - rear of the gearbox or its components denotes the 'in car' position, that is at the flywheel/differential/bellhousing end.

2 Gearshift lever and linkage - adjustment and overhaul

1   If the gears fail to engage properly, adjustment of the gearshift lever may be required. Always check this before assuming that the fault lies within the gearbox.
2   Working inside the car, slacken the screws which secure the gearshift lever support to the centre tunnel. The screw holes are elongated to enable the lever support to be moved fore or aft (Fig. 6.2).
3   Move the lever support forward if lack of engagement has been evident with 1st or 3rd gears.

4   Move the lever support to the rear if it has been found that 2nd, 4th or reverse gears have not been engaging correctly.
5   Re-tighten the lever support screws and check engagement of the gears on the road.
6   To renew worn components, unscrew the self-locking nut which secures the gearshift lever to its support (Fig. 6.3). The ball, socket or spring can be renewed if any of them are worn or damaged.
7   The connecting linkage under the car incorporates a link with flexible joint which may require renewal if it has deteriorated (Fig. 6.4).
8   Reassembly is a reversal of dismantling, but always apply grease to the shift lever ball and socket and to the other linkage rubbing surfaces.

3 Gearbox/final drive - removal and installation

1   Place the car over an inspection pit or raise the rear end by backing it up a pair of ramps. Alternatively, jack-up the rear of the car and support it securely on axle stands placed under the body frame side members. Check that the clearance under the rear of the car is in excess of the diameter of the clutch bellhousing, otherwise the gearbox cannot be withdrawn from under the car.
2   Disconnect the flanges at the outer ends of the driveshafts by unscrewing and removing the securing bolts.
3   Disconnect the clutch operating cable from the release lever on the clutch bellhousing and then release the outer conduit from its support bracket.

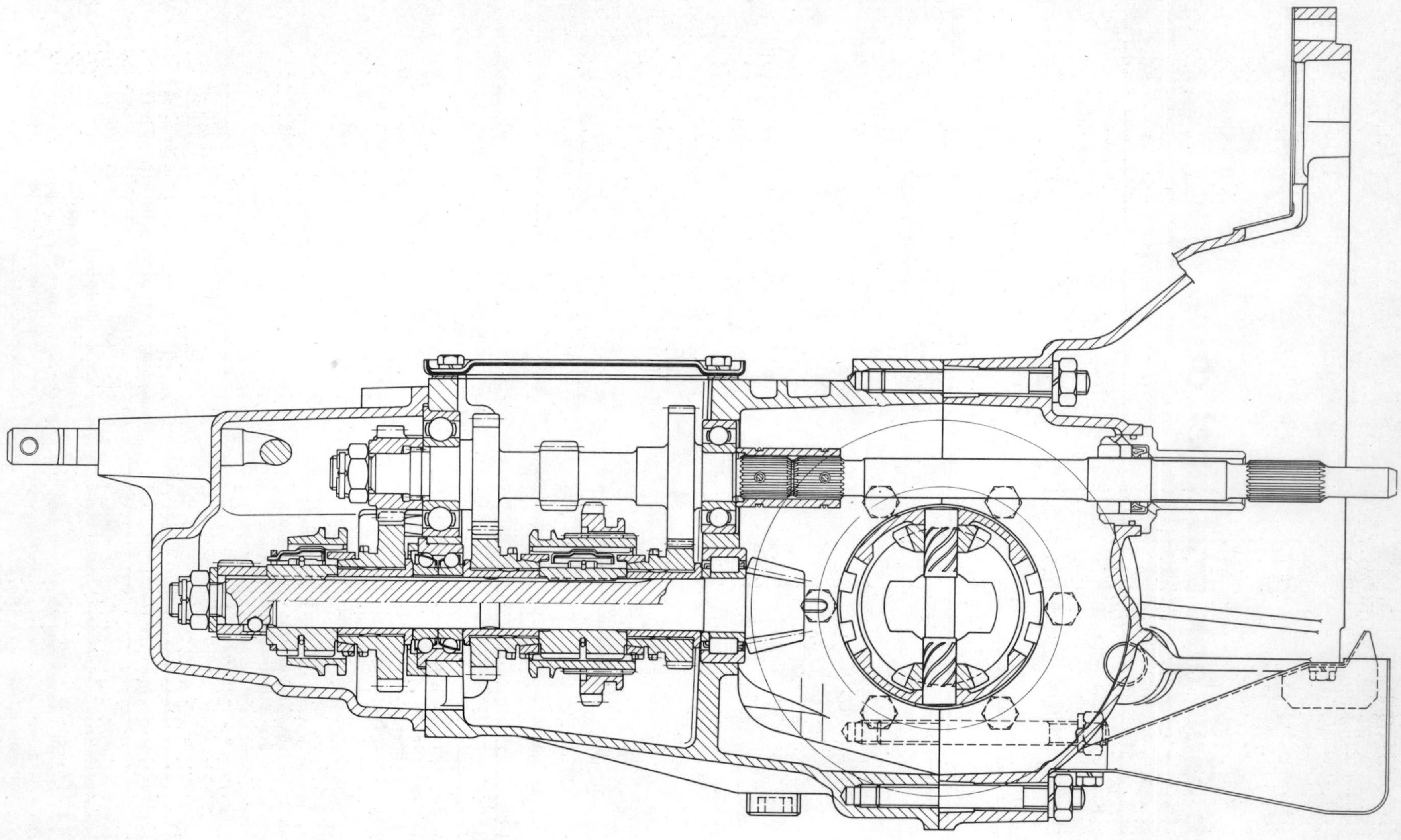

Fig. 6.1. Sectional view of transmission unit

Fig. 6.2. Gearshift lever support bracket

Fig. 6.3. Gearshift lever support and self-locking nut

Fig. 6.4. Gearshift linkage under car

1   Remote control rod
2   Link with flexible joint
3   Connecting rod to gearshift
    lever
4   Flexible boot
5   Shouldered bolts

4   Unhook the clutch release lever return spring.
5   Disconnect the battery negative lead and then remove the front support plate from the starter motor. This is secured under one of the driveshaft inner flange bolts which attach the flange to the gear casing. Disconnect the leads from the starter motor and unbolt and remove the starter.
6   Still working beneath the car, unbolt and remove the long tapering torsion plate from the bottom of the gearbox and from the body-frame box member (photo).
7   Reach up at the rear of the gearbox extension housing and disconnect the speedometer cable by unscrewing the knurled ring (photo).
8   Disconnect the gearshift flexible link from the gearbox remote control rod by removing the special shouldered bolt (photo).
9   Support the engine sump on a jack and a wooden block as an insulator and then place a second jack under the gearbox.
10 Unbolt and remove the 'U' shaped support bracket (complete with flexible mounting pads) from its attachment to the bodyframe (photo).
11 Unscrew and remove the bolts which secure the clutch bellhousing to the engine. Some of these are accessible from below the car while the others are reached from within the engine compartment.
12 Lower the two jacks simultaneously so that the rear of the gearbox is below the floor pan and then withdraw the gearbox towards the front of the car, making sure that the outer ends of the two drive-shafts are depressed rearwards and down to clear the undersides of the suspension lower arms. On no account allow the weight of the gearbox to hang upon the input shaft while the latter is still engaged with the clutch mechanism (Fig. 6.5).
13 Installation is a reversal of removal, but if the clutch mechanism has been dismantled, make sure that the driven plate has been centralised as described in Chapter 5. Check and adjust the clutch pedal free-movement also as described in that Chapter.

Fig. 6.5. Removing gearbox/final drive from under car in a forward direction

3.6 Gearbox torsion plate

 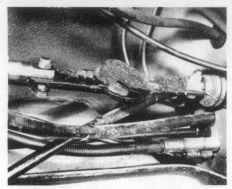 

3.7 Speedometer cable connection to gearbox

3.8 Gearshift flexible link

3.10 Gearbox U-shaped support bracket

4 Gearbox - dismantling and inspection

1 With the gearbox removed from the car, drain the oil and then unbolt and remove the top cover.
2 Within the bellhousing, extract the spring clips and remove the clutch release bearing.
3 Mark the position of the driveshaft inner flanges in relation to the gear case.
4 Unscrew the bolts which secure the oil sealing boots at the inner ends of the driveshafts.
5 Withdraw the locking ring now exposed (photo).
6 Mark the position of the adjuster in relation to the bearing retainer.
7 Unscrew and remove the nuts which secure the bearing retainers and then prise the retainers from the gear case. Slide the inner flange components down the driveshafts (photo).
8 Unscrew and remove the six bolts from within the clutch bell-housing and separate the bellhousing from the gear case.
9 Lift the differential complete with driveshafts from the gearcase.
10 Extract the circlip from the rear end of the input shaft, push out the lockpin and withdraw the input shaft from the gearcase (Fig. 6.6).
11 Unscrew and remove the single retaining bolt and withdraw the speedometer driven gear assembly (photo).
12 Unbolt and remove the extension housing.
13 Withdraw the gearshift remote control rod from the extension housing.
14 Unbolt and remove the 'U' shaped support complete with flexible mountings, from the gear case.
15 Unbolt and remove the plate and gasket which covers the detent springs.
16 Extract the three detent springs and balls.
17 Pull out the split pins from the castellated nuts on the ends of the countershaft and the pinion shaft..
18 Unscrew and remove the locking bolt from reverse shift fork.
19 Push 3rd/4th selector shaft to engage 3rd gear and then move reverse shift fork to lock up the gears in the box so that the pinion and countershaft nuts can be unscrewed. With the gearbox in its normally installed attitude, the upper selector shaft is REVERSE, the middle one is 3rd/4th, and the lower one is 1st/2nd.
20 Unscrew and remove the two shaft castellated nuts.
21 Move the 3rd/4th selector shaft and the reverse shift fork back to their original positions so that the gearbox will again be in the neutral

mode.
22 Unscrew and remove the locking bolts from the remaining shift forks.
23 Withdraw 2nd gear from the end of the countershaft (Fig. 6.7).
24 Withdraw 3rd/4th selector shaft but catching the interlock plungers as it is removed.
25 With draw the speedometer drive gear from the pinion shaft and pick out the locking ball from the depression in the shaft.
26 Withdraw the 2nd gear synchro unit complete with 1st/2nd selector shaft and shift fork from the pinion shaft. Make sure the synchro unit is kept in engagement otherwise it will fall to pieces and have to be reassembled (photo).
27 Turn the gearbox on its side and shake out the remaining interlock plungers.
28 Using two screwdrivers, lever out the counterhsaft front bearing.
29 Remove the countershaft rear bearing and then withdraw the countershaft.
30 Unscrew and remove the locking bolt from the side of reverse idler shaft and then tap the shaft out towards the front of the gearbox and remove the reverse idler gear from it.
31 Stand the gearbox on its front face and withdraw the pinion shaft. Retain any shims and the thrust washers which are fitted behind the pinion shaft rear bearing.
32 Remove the gears which remain in the gearcase.
33 Remove the pinion shaft front bearing assembly which comprises two races and an outer track. This is achieved by removing the two countersunk screws with an impact screwdriver.
34 With the gearbox completely dismantled, clean all components in a suitable solvent and check the gear teeth for wear or chipping and the shafts for scoring.
35 Inspect the gearcase for cracks especially around the bolt and stud holes.
36 Check the bearings for noisy operation when turned with the fingers.
37 Renew the synchroniser units if noisy gearchanges have been evident or the synchromesh could be easily 'beaten' when changing gear.
38 Any faults arising from this examination should be overcome by renewal of the components concerned.
39 Any wear in the pinion shaft can only be rectified by installing a new matched set of pinion shaft and crownwheel, as described in Section 6.

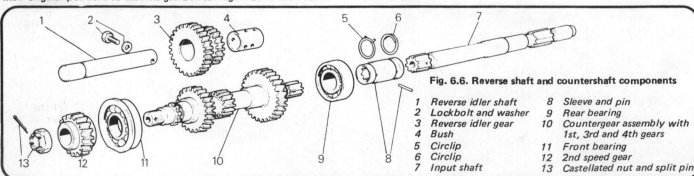

Fig. 6.6. Reverse shaft and countershaft components

1	Reverse idler shaft	8	Sleeve and pin
2	Lockbolt and washer	9	Rear bearing
3	Reverse idler gear	10	Countergear assembly with 1st, 3rd and 4th gears
4	Bush		
5	Circlip	11	Front bearing
6	Circlip	12	2nd speed gear
7	Input shaft	13	Castellated nut and split pin

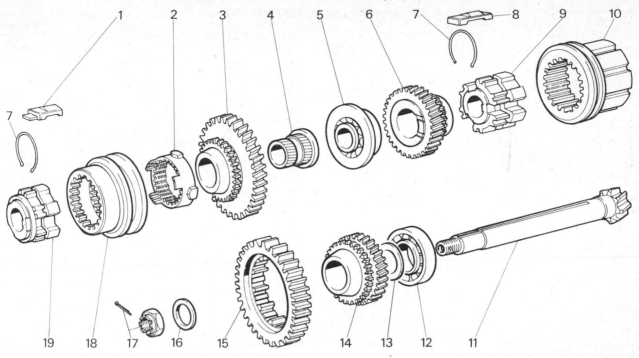

Fig. 6.7. Pinion shaft components

1 Synchro sliding key	6 3rd speed driven gear	11 Pinion shaft	16 Plain washer
2 2nd speed synchro ring	7 Synchro spring	12 Rear bearing	17 Castellated nut and split pin
3 2nd speed driven gear	8 Sliding key	13 Adjustment shim	18 2nd speed synchro sleeve
4 Bush	9 3rd/4th synchro hub	14 4th speed driven gear	19 2nd speed synchro hub
5 Front bearing	10 3rd/4th synchro sleeve	15 1st/reverse gear	

4.5 Driveshaft bearing retainer and adjuster lockring

4.7 Driveshaft inner flange components

4.11 Speedometer driven gear assembly

4.26 2nd gear and synchro unit

5 Gearbox - reassembly

1   During reassembly, lubricate the components with the specified gear oil.

2   Lower the pinion shaft gear train (correctly assembled) into the bottom of the gearcase (Fig. 6.8 and photo).

3   Install the pinion shaft complete with bearing and bushes and the original shims (photos).

4   Install the bearing to the front end of the pinion shaft (photo).

5   Install the bearing retainer noting that the position of the cutout on the retainer is provided to allow installation of the countershaft bearing (photo).

6   Tighten the retainer countersunk screws using an impact screwdriver. If this tool is not available, use a heavy screwdriver and apply leverage to the shaft of the screwdriver with a Stillson wrench.

7 Install 3rd/4th and 1st gear shift forks so that they are located in the grooves of their synchro sleeves (photo).
8 Install the countershaft assembly (photo).
9 Install the countershaft bearings (photos).
10 Fit 2nd gear to the part of the countershaft which lies outside the main gearcase (photo).
11 Screw the castellated nut onto the front end of the countershaft using the fingers to do this.
12 Fit 2nd gear synchro unit to the front end of the pinion shaft and at the same time install the 1st/2nd selector shaft and 2nd gear shift fork, the latter taking up a position outside the main gearcase (photo).
13 Locate the locking ball and fit the speedometer drive gear to the front end of the pinion shaft (photo).
14 Fit the plain washer and then screw the castellated nut onto the front end of the pinion shaft.
15 Screw in and tighten the 1st gear shift fork lock bolt.
16 Drop in the interlock plunger which locates between 1st/2nd and 3rd/4th selector shafts (photo).
17 Install the relay interlock plunger into its hole in the 3rd/4th selector shaft. Use a dab of thick grease to retain it (photo).
18 Install 3rd/4th selector shaft, passing it through the 3rd/4th shift fork in the process (photo).
19 Screw in and tighten the lockbolt which secures 3rd/4th shift fork to its selector shaft (photo).
20 Install the reverse idler shaft and gear (photo).
21 Screw in and tighten reverse idler shaft lockbolt from outside the gearcase.
22 Insert the interlock plunger which locates between reverse and 3rd/4th selector shafts.
23 Install reverse gearshift fork and selector rod but do not screw in its lockbolt at this stage as the shift fork must be free to move when the gears are to be locked up later in order to tighten the pinion shaft and countershaft castellated nuts (photo).
24 Insert the three detent balls into the holes in the side of the gearcase (photo).
25 Insert the three detent springs and then fit the retaining plate and gasket. Use only one bolt to retain the plate (photo).

26 Now fit the 'U' shaped support complete with flexible mountings so that the second bolt which retains the detent spring cover plate can be screwed in. This also acts as a securing bolt for the 'U' shaped support.
27 Lock the gears by moving 3rd/4th selector shaft to engage 3rd gear and then push the (still free) reverse shift fork to lock up the gears in the box.
28 Tighten the pinion and countershaft castellated nuts to the specified torque and insert new split pins (photos).
29 Unlock the gears and then screw in and tighten the lock bolt on the reverse shift fork.
30 Fit a new extension housing gasket.
31 Install the gearshift remote control rod into the extension housing, noting the sealing 'O' ring in the rod groove (photo).
32 Install the extension housing to the gearcase making sure that the dog on the remote control rod engages correctly with the cutouts in the ends of the selector shafts (photo).
33 Screw on and tighten the extension housing nuts and bolts.
34 Fit the gearbox top cover using a new gasket (photo).
35 Fit the input shaft to the rear end of the countershaft so that the splines engage and the lockpin can be pushed into place. Push the locking clip into its groove so that it retains the lockpin (photo).
36 Install the differential complete with driveshafts into the gearcase (photo).
37 Smear the mating faces of the clutch bellhousing and the gearcase with jointing compound and position the two together.
38 Screw in the bolts which secure the bellhousing and the gearcase together noting that the bolts are of two different lengths (photo).
39 Refit the inner flanges of the driveshafts noting that there are sealing 'O' rings on the bearing housings. Make sure that all marks made before dismantling are in alignment. This is particularly important with the bearing adjuster rings (photo).
40 Install the clutch release bearing and the spring clip and return spring to the release lever.
41 The gearbox is now ready to be refitted to the car and it is best to wait until it is installed before filling it with the correct grade and quantity of oil.

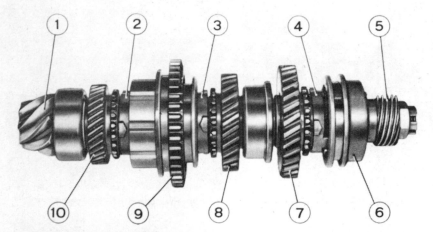

Fig. 6.8. Pinion shaft with gears correctly assembled

1 Pinion
2 4th speed synchro ring
3 3rd speed synchro ring
4 2nd speed synchro ring
5 Speedometer drive gear
6 2nd speed synchro sleeve
7 2nd speed driven gear
8 3rd speed driven gear
9 1st/reverse gear
10 4th speed driven gear

5.2 Pinion shaft geartrain in bottom of casing

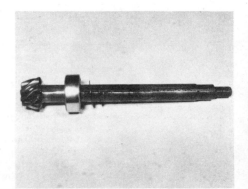

5.3a Pinion shaft with bearing and shims

5.3b Installing pinion shaft

5.4 Installing pinion shaft bearing

5.5 Installing pinion shaft bearing retainer

5.7 3rd/4th and 1st gearshift forks installed

5.8 Countershaft assembly installed

5.9a Countershaft rear bearing installed

5.9b Countershaft front bearing (upper) installed

5.10 2nd gear installed to countershaft

5.12 2nd gear synchro unit, 1st/2nd selector shaft and 2nd gearshift fork fitted to front end of pinion shaft

5.13 Locking ball and speedometer drivegear

5.16 Inserting interlock plunger between 1st/2nd and 3rd/4th selector shafts

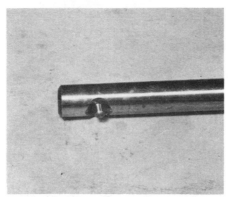

5.17 Relay interlock plunger fitted to 3rd/4th selector shaft

5.18 Installing 3rd/4th selector shaft

5.19 Tightening 3rd/4th shift fork lock bolt

5.20 Installing reverse idler shaft and gear

5.23 Installing reverse gearshift fork and selector shaft

5.24 Detent balls installed

5.25 Detent springs installed

5.28a Tightening pinion shaft castellated nut

5.28b Pinion shaft and countershaft nuts tightened and locked with split pins

5.31 Gearshift remote control rod installed

5.32 Installing extension housing

5.34 Installing top cover

5.35 Fitting input shaft lock pin

5.36 Installing differential/driveshaft assembly

6 Final drive - overhaul and adjustment

1 In the event of wear or excessive noise occurring in the differential assembly, it is recommended that the components are renewed by your Fiat dealer as the meshing of crownwheel and pinion shaft requires the use of special tools and gauges.

2 If any of the gears or bushes on the pinion shaft have been renewed then have your Fiat dealer determine the thickness of the shims which are required between the shaft rear roller bearing and the 4th gear bush. To be able to do this, he will require the new pinion shaft, all the pinion shaft components and the gearcase.

3 If only the pinion shaft and crownwheel are to be renewed (supplied in matched sets) or any other differential components then proceed in the following way.

4 Remove the pinion shaft, as described in Section 4.

5 On the end of the pinion shaft will be found two sets of figures. The upper ones are the matching numbers repeated on the crownwheel while the lower ones indicate the differential (+ or −) between the nominal distance of 2.95 in (75 mm) from the centre-line of the differential to the shoulder at the back of the pinion gearteeth.

6 Compare the lower sets of figures on the old and new pinion shafts and by simple calculation, increase or decrease the thickness of the shims required. Shims are available in thicknesses from 0.0039 to 0.0059 in (0.10 to 0.15 mm).

7 Install the pinion shaft, new shims and gear components, as described in Section 5.

8 To dismantle the differential case and crownwheel, first remove it complete with driveshafts from the gearcase, as described in Section 4, paragraphs 1 to 9.

9 Unscrew and remove the bolts which secure the crownwheel to the differential case.

10 Remove the crownwheel and then slide off the side gear followed by the joint blocks (photo).

11 Withdraw the driveshaft.

12 The opposite driveshaft can be removed after bending up the tabs of the pinion shaft retainer and sliding the retainer from the differential case.

13 Remove the planet gears and differential pinion shaft (photo).

14 Renew any worn components and the bearings if they appear rough or noisy when turned with the fingers.

15 On no account interchange any of the original components from one side of the differential unit to the other.

16 If a new crownwheel is being fitted, make sure that the numbers engraved upon it match those on the pinion shaft.

17 Reassemble the differential case and driveshafts by reversing the dismantling procedure. Make sure that the lubrication channels on the joint blocks are against the inside faces of the grooves in the side gears.

18 Provided the differential side gears and differential case have not been changed, the original side gear thrust washers can be refitted. Where these components have been renewed then it may be necessary to alter the thickness of the thrust washers in order to obtain a turning torque of the differential gears of between 2 and 5 lb f ft (3 and 7 Nm). Use a suitable torque gauge or spring balance to check this. Thrust washers are available in the following thicknesses:

0.027 - 0.031 - 0.035 - 0.039 - 0.043 - 0.047 - 0.051 in (0.7 - 0.8 - 0.9 - 1.0 - 1.1 - 1.2 - 1.3 mm).

19 Tighten the crownwheel bolts to the specified torque wrench setting and remember to bend down the locking tabs of the differential pinion shaft retainer.

20 Install the differential assembly into the gearcase.

21 Install the clutch bellhousing, having applied jointing compound to the mating flanges of the gearcase and bellhousing, and then tighten the securing bolts to the specified torque.

22 If the original components are being refitted then set the side adjusters to their original (marked) positions.

23 If new components have been fitted, a dial gauge should be used to check the backlash between the teeth of the gearbox pinion shaft and the teeth of the crownwheel. The backlash should be between 0.003 and 0.005 in (0.08 and 0.13 mm). Turn the bearing side adjusters to obtain the specified backlash. In the absence of the correct wrench, use a pair of narrow-nosed pliers to turn the adjusters (Fig. 6.10).

24 Now the turning torque of the differential roller bearings must be checked. Using either a spring balance and cord attached to a drive-shaft or a torque gauge, the force required to rotate the bearings should be between 1 and 1.5 lb f ft (1.3 and 1.95 Nm). If a correction is needed, move one adjuster slightly in the appropriate direction and then turn the other adjuster in the opposite direction. Failure to do this will upset the previously set backlash.

25 With the final drive assembly correctly set, fit the driveshaft inner flanges with new 'O' ring seals, and then the adjuster lock rings taking care not to alter the position of the adjusters.

26 Fit the oil retaining boots and their retaining flanges. Make sure that the driveshaft inner oil seals and retainers are in good condition.

5.38 Tightening a clutch bellhousing to gearcase bolt

5.39 Refitting a driveshaft inner flange

6.10 Differential side gear, driveshaft and joint blocks

6.13 View of planet gears and a differential side gear (driveshaft removed)

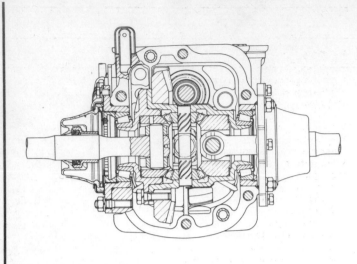

Fig. 6.9. Cross-sectional view of final drive/differential

Fig. 6.10. Using a dial gauge to check crownwheel backlash. Probe of dial gauge passes through input shaft hole in bellhousing to contact crownwheel tooth

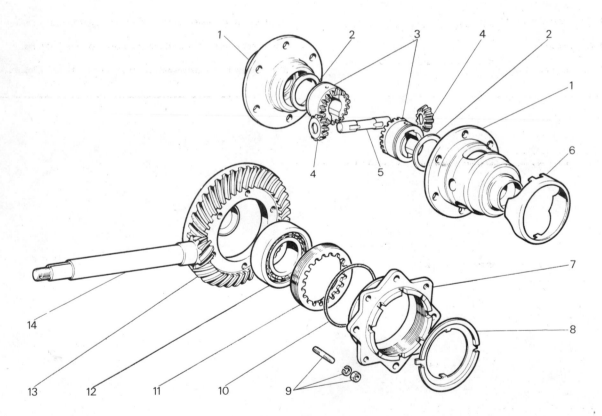

Fig. 6.11. Exploded view of the final drive/differential

1	Differential case	5	Differential pinion shaft	8	Bearing adjuster lock ring
2	Side gear thrust washer	6	Differential pinion shaft	9	Stud, nut and washer
3	Side gears		retainer	10	'O' ring
4	Differential pinions	7	Bearing housing	11	Adjuster

12	Roller bearing
13	Crownwheel
14	Pinion shaft

7 Fault diagnosis - gearbox

Symptom	Reason/s
Weak or ineffective synchromesh	Synchro. cones worn or damaged. Baulk rings worn. Defective synchro unit.
Jumps out of gear	Worn interlock plunger. Worn detent ball. Weak or broken detent spring. Worn shift fork or synchro sleeve groove. Worn gear.
Excessive noise	Incorrect oil grade. Oil level too low. Worn gear teeth. Worn pinion shaft bearings. Worn thrust washers. Worn input or pinion shaft splines.
Difficult gear changing or selection	Incorrect clutch free-movement.

8 Fault diagnosis - final drive and differential

Symptom	Reason/s
Noisy differential: a) During normal running	Lack of oil, damaged or worn gears, incorrect adjustment.
b) During deceleration	Incorrect adjustment or damage to drive pinion bearings.
c) During turning of vehicle	Worn or damaged driveshaft bearing, worn differential gears.

Chapter 7 Driveshafts and rear hubs

Contents

Specifications

Torque wrench settings		lb f ft	Nm
Driveshaft outer flange to flexible joint		18	25
Driveshaft inner flange to gearcase		11	15

1 General description

1 The driveshafts are of open type, having a sliding joint at their inner ends and a flexible joint at their outer ends (Fig. 7.1).
2 Power is transmitted from the differential side gears through the driveshafts to the outer flexible joints which are in turn splined to short axle stubs which run in double taper roller hub bearings (Fig. 7.2).
3 The brake drums are bolted to the flanges on the outer ends of these axle stubs and the roadwheels are bolted to the brake drums.

2 Driveshaft - joint seals and boots - removal and refitting

1 Place the car over an inspection pit or on ramps to provide access to the underside of the car.
2 Unscrew and remove the four bolts which secure the driveshaft outer flange to the flexible joint (photo).
3 Disconnect the outer flange from the flexible joint. Take care not to lose the small coil spring from inside the end of the driveshaft (photos).
4 Mark the relative positions of the driveshaft inner flange to the gearcase also the oil sealing boot retainer to the inner flange. Unbolt the driveshaft inner flange boot retainer (photo).
5 Extract the circlip from the outer end of the driveshaft and slide off the outer joint, the flexible boot followed by the flexible boot retainer from the inner end of the driveshaft, the boot itself, the oil seal and seal retainer.
6 Renew any worn seals or split flexible boots. The seal/sleeve assembly can be prised out of the inner flexible boot (photo).
7 Reassembly and refitting are reversals of removal and dismantling.

3 Driveshafts - removal and installation

1 Remove the gearbox complete with driveshafts, as described in Section 3, Chapter 6.
2 Remove the final drive/differential and driveshafts from the gearcase, as described in Section 4, paragraphs 1 to 9 of Chapter 6.
3 The crownwheel must now be unbolted and the driveshafts removed, as described in Section 6, paragraphs 8 to 12 of Chapter 6.
4 Installation is a reversal of removal, but tighten the crownwheel bolts to the specified torque of 33 lb f ft (46 Nm), make sure that the grooves in the joint blocks are in contact with the inner faces of the channels in the side gears to provide proper lubrication and that the

tabs of the differential pinion shaft retainer are correctly bent down.

4 Rear hub and axle stubs - dismantling, reassembly and adjustment

1 Disconnect the outer flanges of the driveshaft from the flexible joint by unscrewing and removing the four securing bolts.
2 Push the driveshaft to one side to expose the staked nut on the inner end of the axle stub.
3 Relieve the staking on the nut, apply the handbrake fully and unscrew the nut.
4 Jack-up the rear of the car and support it securely under the bodyframe side members and the suspension arm.
5 Remove the roadwheels.
6 Release the handbrake and unbolt and remove the brake drum.
7 Tap the axle stub out of the hub bearings, taking great care not to damage the threads at the inner end of the stub. Use a brass drift or screw an old nut for a few threads to take the impact of the hammer blows.
8 With the axle stub removed, prise out the outer oil seal, extract the spacer and circlip and remove the outer tapered roller bearing race.
9 Repeat the removal operations for the inner oil seal and circlip and inner tapered roller bearing.
10 If the bearings are in good condition, pack them with fresh multi-purpose grease and reassemble using new inner and outer oil seals.
11 If the bearings must be renewed due to wear, extract the collapsible spacer and discard it, then drive out the bearing outer tracks.
12 Drive in the new bearing outer tracks, fit a new collapsible spacer, fit the tapered roller bearings, the circlips, outer spacer and new inner and outer oil seals. Make sure that the new bearings are well packed with grease but not over lubricated.
13 Install the axle stub and screw on a new nut finger-tight.
14 Refit the brake drum and then wind a cord round the outside of the drum and attach it to a spring balance.
15 The nut on the inner end of the axle stub must now be tightened a fraction of a turn at a time until the pull required to start the brake drum turning is 1 lb. (0.45 kg) as recorded on the spring balance. On no account back off the nut in an attempt to rectify overtightening as the compressible spacer will have been over-compressed and a new one must be fitted and the adjustment started all over again.
16 When adjustment is correct, stake the nut, reconnect the driveshaft, having first applied plenty of grease to the axle stub splines and to the little coil spring which is located in the end of the driveshaft coupling flange.
17 Refit the roadwheel and lower the car to the ground.

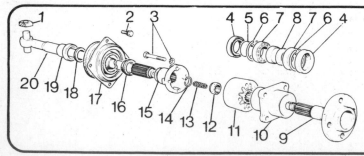

Fig. 7.1. Driveshaft and rear hub components

1	Joint block	11	Flexible joint
2	Driveshaft inner flange bolt	12	Axle stub nut
3	Driveshaft outer flange bolt	13	Spring
4	Hub oil seals	14	Circlip
5	Spacer	15	Outer coupling flange
6	Circlips	16	Flexible boot sleeve
7	Roller bearings	17	Inner boot retainer
8	Collapsible spacer	18	Oil seal
9	Axle stub	19	Oil seal retainer
10	Hub	20	Driveshaft

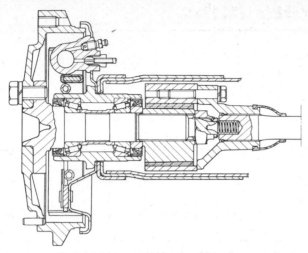

Fig. 7.2. Sectional view of a rear hub

Fig. 7.3. Withdrawing an axle stub from a rear wheel hub

2.1 Removing driveshaft outer coupling flange bolts

2.3a Driveshaft outer flexible coupling

2.3b Outer end of driveshaft showing coupling flange and internal spring (well greased)

2.4 Driveshaft inner flexible boot

2.6a Driveshaft inner flexible boot with oil seal/sleeve

2.6b Oil seal/sleeve removed from driveshaft inner flexible boot

5 Fault diagnosis - driveshafts and rear hubs

Symptom	Reason/s
Noisy rear hub	Worn bearings. Incorrect adjustment. Buckled roadwheel. Defective tyre/s Worn splines on axle stub.
'Clunk' on taking up drive or on overrun	Worn shaft splines. Loose flange bolts. Worn grooves in side gear.

Chapter 8 Braking system

Contents

Specifications

System	Hydraulic, four wheel drum dual circuit. Handbrake mechanical to rear wheels
Drum diameter	6.697 to 6.708 in (170.1 to 170.4 mm)
Maximum increase in internal diameter after refacing	0.04 in (1 mm)
Brake lining dimension	7.08 x 1.18 x 0.17 in (180.0 x 30.0 x 4.3 mm)
Minimum lining thickness before renewal	0.059 in (1.5 mm)
Master cylinder bore (diameter)	0.75 in (19.05 mm)

Wheel cylinder bore (diameter)

Front	15/16 in (23.80 mm)
Rear	5/8 in (15.70 mm)

Torque wrench settings	lb f ft	Nm
Rear drum securing bolt	60	83
Rear brake backplate	40	55
Master cylinder flange nut	12	16
Wheel cylinder to backplate bolt	7	10

1 General description

1 The braking system is of hydraulic, dual circuit, four wheel drum type with the handbrake operating mechanically on the rear wheels only (Fig. 8.1).
2 All brakes incorporate self-adjusting shoes.
3 The master cylinder is mounted on the front bulkhead just below the luggage compartment floor and adjacent to the steering box.
4 The fluid reservoir is located within the luggage boot.
5 A pendant type footbrake pedal is used with a stoplamp switch mounted on the pedal support bracket (photo).

2 Brake shoes - description of automatic adjusters

1 The automatic adjustment of the brake shoes is based upon the following arrangement.
2 Each shoe is located on a steady post (which is secured to the backplate) by means of a blind bush (Fig. 8.4).
3 The hole in the shoe web is larger in diameter than the outside diameter of the bush and the internal diameter of the bush is larger

than the diameter of the steady post.
4 When the brakes are applied, the shoes move outward into contact with the drum which also allows the web of the shoe to slide in relation to the bush.
5 Through an assembly of friction washers and a heavy coil spring, the shoe does not fully return when the brake pedal is released, but the shoe lining retracts from the drum only by the clearance which exists between the steady post and the bore of the bush, so providing minimum lining to drum clearance with short pedal travel.
6 It will be appreciated that the system depends upon the pressure of the coil springs being greater than the retracting tension of the shoe return springs and this will normally apply unless the friction washers or shoe web have become contaminated with oil or grease.
7 **On no account apply oil to the friction washers or shoe web during brake overhaul.**
8 It has been found in practice that after a distance of about 4,000 miles (6,400 km) has been covered, the efficiency of the automatic adjustment device leaves something to be desired and this is indicated by lengthening of the foot brake pedal travel. When this occurs, drive the car in reverse gear and apply the brakes very sharply. This will bring the shoes back to the closest adjustment. Repeat periodically if the need arises.

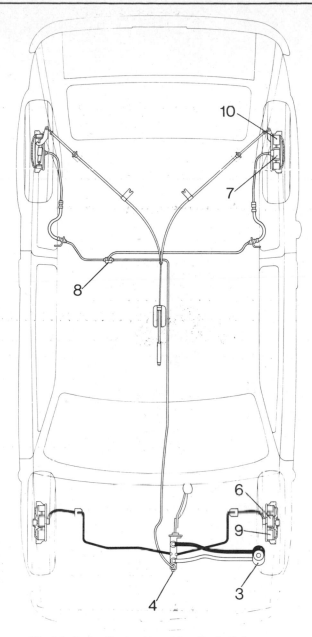

Fig. 8.1. Hydraulic circuits and handbrake linkage

3	Fluid reservoir	8	Three way connector
4	Master cylinder	9	Brake shoes
6	Wheel cylinder	10	Brake shoes
7	Wheel cylinder		

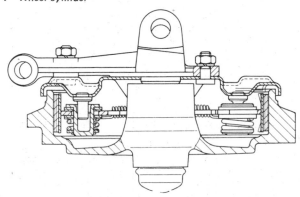

Fig. 8.2. Cut away view of a front brake assembly

3 Brake shoes - inspection and renewal

Front brakes

1   Jack-up the front of the car and support it securely.
2   Remove the roadwheel.
3   Tap off the grease cap and then relieve the staking on the nut at the end of the stub axle.
4   Unscrew and remove the nut and take off the thrust washer. The nut on the right-hand stub axle has a left-hand thread.
5   Support the weight of the brake drum and pull it directly from the stub axle, catching the outer taper roller bearing as the drum is withdrawn (photo).
6   Brush any accumulations of dust taking care not to inhale it and then inspect the thickness of the friction material. With bonded type linings, renew them if the thickness of the remaining material is 0.06 in (1.5 mm) or less. With rivetted linings, the shoes must be renewed if the linings have worn down to, or nearly down to the rivet heads.
7   To remove the shoes, unhook the shoe retracting springs and lift the shoes from the brake backplate. Twist a piece of wire or engage a rubber band round the wheel cylinder pistons to prevent them falling out while the shoes are missing. On no account depress the brake pedal (photo).
8   A compressor is now required to compress the spring on the shoe self-adjusting mechanism so that the circlip can be extracted. A valve spring compressor will often serve the purpose (Fig. 8.3).
9   Remove the self-adjusting components, keeping them in strict order and then reassemble them to the new shoes (Fig. 8.4).
10 Compress the spring again and engage the circlip (photo).
11 Remove the wire or band from the wheel cylinder pistons, locate the shoes on the brake backplate and reconnect the shoe retracting springs.
12 Refit the brake drum, adjust the hub bearings, as described in Chapter 11, using a new nut on the end of the stub axle and staking it securely.
13 Refit the roadwheel and lower the car to the ground.
14 Repeat the operations on the opposite front wheel.

Rear brakes

15 Jack-up the rear of the car and remove the roadwheels.
16 Unbolt and remove the brake drum (photo).
17 Repeat the operations described in paragraphs 6 to 11 of this Section, noting that the handbrake lever strut must be removed from between the upper ends of the shoe webs (photo).
18 Refit the drum and roadwheel and lower the car to the ground.
19 When all the shoes have been renewed, apply the footbrake several times to position the shoes and actuate the automatic adjuster mechanism.

4 Wheel cylinder - removal, overhaul and refitting

1   Remove the brake drum and shoes, as described in the preceding Section.
2   Disconnect the flexible brake hose at its union with the rigid pipe-line at the support bracket. Plug the open end of the line to prevent loss of fluid.
3   The flexible hose can now be unscrewed from the wheel cylinder.
4   Unbolt and remove the wheel cylinder from the brake backplate.
5   Clean away all external dirt and pull off the boots and extract the pistons (Fig. 8.5).
6   Push out the reaction spring, thrust washers and seals.
7   At this stage inspect the condition of the piston and cylinder surfaces. If they are scored or scratched or show 'bright' wear areas, then renew the wheel cylinder complete.
8   If these components are in good condition, extract the seals and discard them. Clean the components in hydraulic fluid or methylated spirit - nothing else!
9   Obtain a repair kit and manipulate the new seals into position using the fingers only for the purpose.
10 Dip the components in clean hydraulic fluid before assembling them into the cylinder.
11 Refit the boots, the shoes and drum.
12 Reconnect the hydraulic hose and then bleed the circuit, as described in Section 8.

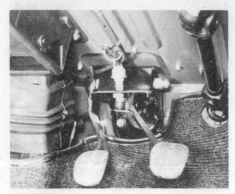

1.5 Brake and clutch pedals showing stop lamp switch

3.5 Front hub outer bearing and thrust washer

3.7 Front brake assembly

3.10 An automatic adjuster showing retaining circlip

3.16 Rear brake drum showing securing bolts

3.17 Rear brake assembly

13 Although the wheel cylinder seals can be renewed without removing the cylinder from the brake backplate, this is not advised; as apart from the possibility of dirt entering the cylinder it is very difficult to inspect the interior of the cylinder, which is essential if the seal has been deformed or cut and has been operating in this condition for any length of time and may have caused the piston to tilt and scrape the cylinder walls.

5 Master cylinder - removal, overhaul and refitting

1 Open the lid of the luggage boot and remove the cover from the boot floor which gives access to the brake master cylinder.
2 Disconnect the fluid supply pipes from the master cylinder and let the fluid drain from the reservoir into a suitable container. Take great care not to let the fluid come into contact with the paintwork as it will act as an effective paint stripper!
3 Disconnect the rigid pipelines from the master cylinder by unscrewing their unions. Cap the open ends of the lines to prevent entry of dirt (Fig. 8.6).
4 Working either through the opening in the luggage boot floor or by raising the front of the car and reaching upwards next to the steering box, unscrew the master cylinder flange mounting nuts and withdraw the unit.
5 Clean away external dirt and then insert a rod into the pushrod hole at the end of the cylinder and depress the pistons two or three times to expel the hydraulic fluid.
6 Secure the master cylinder body in the jaws of a vice and pull off the dust excluder (Fig. 8.7).
7 Depress the pistons against their spring pressure and unscrew and remove the stop bolts. Gently release the pressure applied to the pistons and then extract first the primary piston components followed by the secondary piston components (Fig. 8.8).
8 At this stage, examine the surfaces of the pistons and cylinder bore for scoring or 'bright' wear areas. If these are evident, renew the master cylinder complete.
9 If the components are in good condition, discard the seals and obtain a repair kit which will contain all the renewable components.

Clean each part in hydraulic fluid or methylated spirit - nothing else!
10 Manipulate the new seals into position using the fingers only. Dip the components in clean hydraulic fluid before inserting them into the cylinder.
11 Install the secondary components first and then depress the piston with a rod so that the stop bolt can be screwed into engagement with the secondary piston.
12 Install the primary piston components and again depress the piston so that the second stop bolt can be screwed in. Fit the new dust excluding boot.
13 Refitting is a reversal of removal, but as the master cylinder is offered into position, remember to engage the pedal pushrod into the end of the cylinder body.
14 On completion, bleed both hydraulic circuits, as described in Section 8.

6 Flexible hydraulic hoses - inspection and renewal

1 Inspect the flexible hoses for rubbing, chafing or general deterioration at regular intervals. Bend each hose double with the fingers. If tiny cracks can be seen then the rubber is perished and the hose must be renewed.
2 Disconnect a flexible hose at its union with the rigid brake line at the support bracket.
3 Hold the end fitting on the flexible hose quite still while the union nut is unscrewed. Now using two spanners, unscrew the locknut which secures the flexible hose and fitting to the support bracket.
4 Remove the flexible hose from the end fitting and unscrew it from the wheel cylinder (front brake) or the rigid pipe connecting union (rear brake).
5 When installing a flexible hose, make sure that it takes on a similar curve to that followed by the original one. If necessary, the hose end fitting can be rotated in the support bracket by not more than a quarter turn to achieve this.
6 Always bleed the appropriate hydraulic circuit on completion of the work.

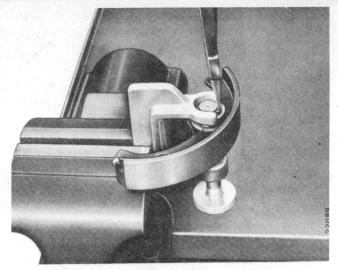

Fig. 8.3. Extracting a circlip from shoe automatic adjuster

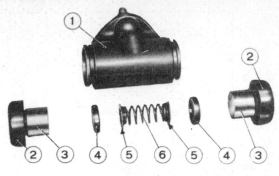

Fig. 8.5. Exploded view of a wheel cylinder

1 Cylinder	4 Seals
2 Boots	5 Thrust washers
3 Pistons	6 Spring

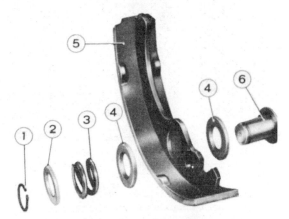

Fig. 8.4. Brake shoe automatic adjuster components

1 Circlip	4 Friction washers
2 Plain washer	5 Brake shoe
3 Spring	6 Blind bush

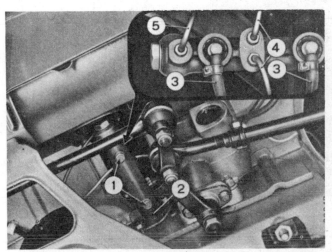

Fig. 8.6. Location of brake master cylinder. Inset, view through luggage boot floor aperture

1 Stop bolts	4 Hydraulic line to front brakes
2 Master cylinder	
3 Fluid feed from reservoir	5 Hydraulic line to rear brakes

Fig. 8.7. Exploded view of the master cylinder

1 Spring washer	14 Secondary piston
2 Fluid feed elbow	15 Seal
3 Seal	16 Spacer
4 Master cylinder body	17 Spring seat
5 End plug	18 Spring
6 Stop bolt	19 Spring cup
7 Seal	20 Spring
8 Spring seat	21 Seal
9 Spring	22 Spacer
10 Spring cup	23 Primary piston
11 Spring	24 Seal
12 Seal	25 Dust excluding boot
13 Spacer	

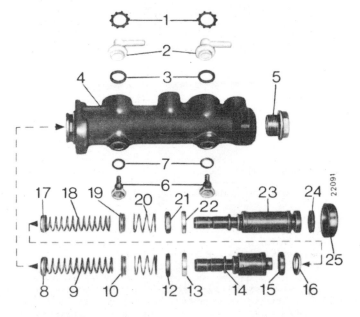

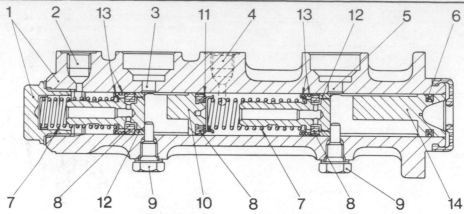

Fig. 8.8. Sectional view of brake master cylinder

1 Master cylinder body and end plug	4 Fluid outlet to front brakes	8 Seal	12 Spacers
2 Fluid outlet to rear brakes	5 Fluid inlet from reservoir	9 Stop bolt	13 Spring and cup
3 Fluid inlet from reservoir	6 Seal	10 Secondary piston	14 Primary piston
	7 Spring	11 Washer	

7 Rigid brake lines - inspection and renewal

1   At regular intervals wipe the steel pipes clean and examine them for signs of rust or denting caused by flying stones.
2   Examine the securing clips. Bend the tongues of the clips if necessary to ensure that they hold the brake pipes securely without letting them rattle or vibrate.
3   Check that the pipes are not touching any adjacent components or rubbing against any part of the vehicle. Where this is observed, bend the pipe gently away to clear.
4   Any section of pipe which is rusty or chafed should be renewed. Brake pipes are available to the correct length and fitted with end unions from most Fiat dealers and can be made to pattern by many accessory suppliers. When installing the new pipes use the old pipes as a guide to bending and do not make any bends sharper than it is necessary.
5   The system will of course have to be bled when the circuit has been reconnected.

8 Hydraulic system - bleeding

1   Removal of all the air from the hydraulic system is essential to the correct working of the braking system, and before undertaking this examine the fluid reservoir cap to ensure that both vent holes, one on top and the second underneath but not in line, are clear; check the level of fluid and top up if required.
2   Check all brake line unions and connections for possible seepage, and at the same time check the condition of the rubber hoses, which may be perished.
3   If the condition of the wheel cylinders is in doubt, check for possible signs of fluid leakage.
4   If there is any possibility of incorrect fluid having been put into the system, drain all the fluid out and flush through with methylated spirit. Renew all piston seals and cups since these will be affected and could possibly fail under pressure.
5   Gather together a clean glass jar, a length of tubing which fits tightly over the bleed nipples, and a tin of the correct brake fluid.
6   To bleed the system if the master cylinder has been disturbed, clean dirt from the bleed nipples and start on the rear brakes by removing the rubber cap over the bleed valve, and fitting a rubber tube in position.
7   Place the end of the tube in a clean glass jar containing sufficient fluid to keep the end of the tube submerged during the operation (Fig. 8.9).
8   Open the bleed valve with a spanner and have an assistant quickly depress the brake pedal. After slowly releasing the pedal, pause for a moment to allow the fluid to recoup in the master cylinder and then depress again. This will force air from the system. Continue until no more air bubbles can be seen coming from the tube. At intervals make certain that the reservoir is kept topped-up otherwise air will enter at this point again.

9   Once the rear brakes have been bled, bleed the front brake furthest from the master cylinder followed by the remaining front brake.
10 Tighten the bleed screws when the pedal is in the fully depressed position.
11 If a component of one hydraulic circuit only has been disturbed, then only that circuit need be bled.
12 Use only clean fluid for topping-up purposes and discard fluid from the bleed jar. Fluid used for topping-up should have been kept in an air tight container and remained unshaken for the previous 24 hours.

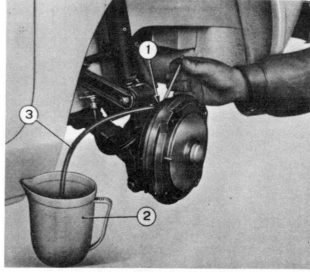

Fig. 8.9. Bleeding a front brake

1 Bleed nipple	3 Bleed tube
2 Container	

9 Brake drum - renovation

1   Whenever a brake drum is removed, examine its shoe lining rubbing surface for scoring or deep grooving.
2   After a considerable mileage the internal diameter of the drum can wear oval in shape due to normal brake application characteristics. This can often be detected by juddering when the brakes are applied although it is known that the system is otherwise in first class condition.
3   Where any of these conditions are encountered, the interior of the drum can be refaced provided that the internal diameter is not increased by more than 0.04 in (1 mm). This is a job for your dealer.
4   Where refacing would create drums of above the maximum internal diameter permissible, fit new ones.

10 Handbrake - adjustment

1 The handbrake should normally be fully on after having passed over for or five teeth of its ratchet (Fig. 8.10).
2 Where handbrake travel is excessive, jack-up the rear of the car so that the roadwheels are free to turn.
3 Apply the handbrake control lever over three notches.
4 Release the locknuts at the cable abutment brackets.
5 Turn the cable adjustment nuts until each roadwheel just locks. Tighten the locknuts.
6 Release the handbrake and check that the two rear roadwheels are free to turn.

11 Handbrake cable - renewal

1 If the handbrake cable should break, or even show signs of age with fraying, it will need changing.
2 Remove the split pin from the pin holding each cable end fork to the lever on the handbrake mechanism on the rear of the brake drums (photo).
3 Having pulled out the pins from the forks undo the adjuster nuts and locknuts from the brackets on the rear suspension swinging arms. These are 'U' shaped brackets. The cable can be pulled along until the inner cable can pass through the slot in the bracket. Disconnect the conduit clamps.
4 Inside the car remove the two small bolts holding the tin cover to the panel just in front of the rear seat. Remove the tunnel trim and the seat.
5 Undo the bolts holding the handbrake bracket to the top of the tunnel. Now pull up the handbrake assembly until the pin through the wheel working the cable can be reached. Take out the split pin, remove the wheel's pin, and disengage the cable from the lever.

6 Disengage the ends of the outer cables from their seats in the holes in the rear bulkhead. Slide them along to the larger holes nearby. Then the cable can be threaded out of the car.
7 When fitting the new cable grease all the pivot pins.
8 Adjust the cable, as described in Section 10.

11.2 Handbrake cable attachment to rear brake

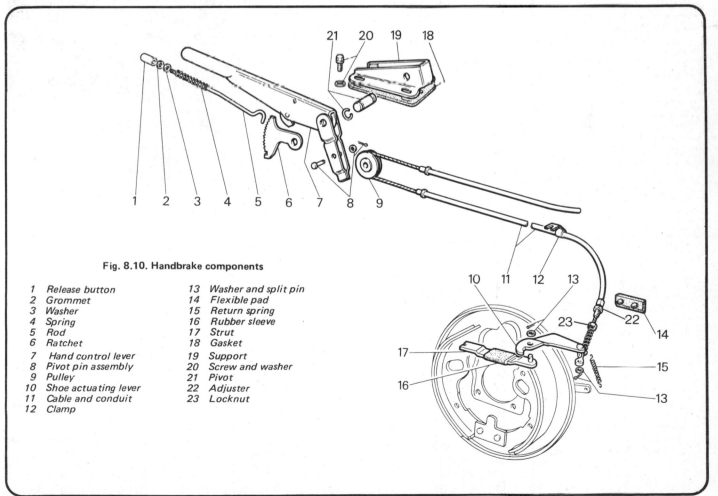

Fig. 8.10. Handbrake components

1	Release button	13	Washer and split pin
2	Grommet	14	Flexible pad
3	Washer	15	Return spring
4	Spring	16	Rubber sleeve
5	Rod	17	Strut
6	Ratchet	18	Gasket
7	Hand control lever	19	Support
8	Pivot pin assembly	20	Screw and washer
9	Pulley	21	Pivot
10	Shoe actuating lever	22	Adjuster
11	Cable and conduit	23	Locknut
12	Clamp		

12 Fault diagnosis - braking system

Symptom	Reason/s
Brake grab	Brake shoe linings not bedded-in. Contaminated with oil or grease. Scored drums.
Brake drag	Master cylinder faulty. Brake foot pedal return impeded. Blocked filler cap vent. Master cylinder reservoir or compartments overfilled. Seized wheel cylinder. Incorrect adjustment of handbrake. Weak or broken shoe return springs. Crushed or blocked pipelines.
Brake pedal feels hard	Friction surfaces contaminated with oil or grease. Glazed friction material surfaces. Seized wheel cylinder.
Excessive pedal travel	Low fluid level in reservoir. Automatic shoe adjusters faulty. Worn front wheel bearings. System requires bleeding. Worn linings.
Pedal creep during sustained application	Fluid leak. Faulty master cylinder.
Pedal 'spongy' or 'springy'	System requires bleeding. Perished flexible hose. Loose master cylinder. Cracked brake drum. Linings not bedded-in. Faulty master cylinder.
Fall in master cylinder fluid level	Normal lining wear. Leak.

Chapter 9 Electrical system

Contents

Specifications

System type	12V negative earth
Battery	12V 34 A/h

Dynamo
Type	Fiat DSV 90/12/16/3S
Maximum steady output	230W
Maximum steady current	16A
Charing starts	120 rev/min (17 mph - 27 km/h in top gear)
Armature resistance	68°F (20°C) 0.145 ± 0.01 ohm
Field winding resistance	68°F (20°C) 7.7 to 8.1 ohm

Regulator unit
Type	Fiat GN 2/12/16

Starter motor
Type	Fiat B 76-05/12S pre-engaged
Rated output	0.5 kW

Fuses

Number	Rating (Amps)	Circuit protected
1 - A	8	Direction indicators, fuel gauge, stop lamps Windscreen wiper, oil pressure warning lamp
2 - B	8	Horn, interior lamp
3 - C	8	Headlamp (L.H. main beam), main beam warning lamp
4 - D	8	Headlamp (R.H. main beam)
5 - E	8	Headlamp (L.H. dipped beam)
6 - F	8	Headlamp (R.H. dipped beam)
7 - G	8	Front parking lamp (L.H.), tail lamp (R.H.), rear number plate lamp (L.H.)
8 - H	8	Front parking lamp (R.H.), instrument panel lamps, tail lamps (L.H.) number plate lamp (R.H.)

Bulbs

Location	Wattage
Headlamps	45/40W double filament
Front parking and direction indicator lamp	5/21W double filament
Side repeater lamp	4W
Tail and brake stoplamp	5/21W double filament
Rear direction indicator lamp	21W
Rear number plate lamp	5W
Interior lamp	5W
Instrument and parking lamp and indicator lamps	3W
Warning and indicator lamps	1.2W

Torque wrench settings	lb f ft	Nm
Dynamo pulley flange nut	25	35
Fan to dynamo shaft nut	25	35
Dynamo pulley hub nut	100	138

1 General description

1 The electrical system is of 12V negative earth type.
2 The battery is mounted at the front of the car within the luggage compartment (photo).
3 The battery is charged by a dynamo which is driven by a drivebelt from the centrifugal oil filter/pulley which is mounted on the rear end of the crankshaft.
4 A regulator unit controls the charging rate.
5 A pre-engaged starter motor is fitted.

1.2 Location of the battery

2 Battery - removal and installation

1 The battery is located at the front on the right-hand side of the engine compartment.
2 Disconnect the lead from the negative terminal by unscrewing the clamp bolt.
3 Disconnect the lead from the positive terminal and remove the battery securing bolts and frame.
4 Lift the battery carefully from its tray and avoid spilling electrolyte on the paintwork.
5 Installation is a reversal of removal, but when connecting the terminals, clean off any corrosion or white deposits which may be present and when the clamp bolts are tight, smear the terminal and clamp with petroleum jelly to prevent corrosion recurring.

3 Battery - maintenance

1 Carry out the regular weekly maintenance described in the Routine Maintenance Section at the front of this manual.
2 Clean the top of the battery, removing all dirt and moisture.
3 As well as keeping the terminals clean and covered with petroleum jelly, the top of the battery, and especially the top of the cells, should be kept clean and dry. This helps prevent corrosion and ensures that the battery does not become partially discharged by leakage through dampness and dirt.
4 Once every three months, remove the battery and inspect the battery securing bolts, the battery clamp plate, tray and battery leads

for corrosion (white fluffy deposits on the metal which are brittle to touch). If any corrosion is found, clean off the deposits with ammonia and paint over the clean metal with an anti-rust/anti-acid paint.
5 At the same time inspect the battery case for cracks. If a crack is found, clean and plug it with one of the proprietary compounds marketed for this purpose. If leakage through the crack has been excessive then it will be necessary to refill the appropriate cell with fresh electrolyte as detailed later. Cracks are frequently caused to the top of the battery cases by pouring in distilled water in the middle of winter *after* instead of *before* a run. This gives the water no chance to mix with the electrolyte and so the former freezes and splits the battery case.
6 If topping-up the battery becomes excessive and the case has been inspected for cracks that could cause leakage, but none are found, the battery is being over-charged and the voltage regulator will have to be checked and reset.
7 With the battery on the bench at the three monthly interval check, measure its specific gravity with a hydrometer to determine the state of charge and condition of the electrolyte (Fig. 9.1). There should be very little variation between the different cells and if a variation in excess of 0.025 is present it will be due to either:

 a) *Loss of electrolyte from the battery at some time caused by spillage or a leak, resulting in a drop in the specific gravity of electrolyte when the deficiency was replaced with distilled water instead of fresh electrolyte.*
 b) *An internal short circuit caused by buckling of the plates or a similar malady pointing to the likelihood of total battery failure in the near future.*

8 The specific gravity of the electrolyte for fully charged conditions at the electrolyte temperature indicated, is listed in Table A. The specific gravity of a fully discharged battery at different temperatures of the electrolyte is given in Table B.

Table A
Specific Gravity - Battery Fully Charged

1.268 at 100°F or 38°C electrolyte temperature
1.272 at 90°F or 32°C electrolyte temperature
1.276 at 80°F or 27°C electrolyte temperature
1.280 at 70°F or 21°C electrolyte temperature
1.284 at 60°F or 16°C electrolyte temperature
1.288 at 50°F or 10°C electrolyte temperature
1.292 at 40°F or 4°C electrolyte temperature
1.296 at 30°F or -1.5°C electrolyte temperature

Table B
Specific Gravity - Battery Fully Discharged

1.098 at 100°F or 38°C electrolyte temperature
1.102 at 90°F or 32°C electrolyte temperature
1.106 at 80°F or 27°C electrolyte temperature
1.110 at 70°F or 21°C electrolyte temperature
1.114 at 60°F or 16°C electrolyte temperature
1.118 at 50°F or 10°C electrolyte temperature
1.112 at 40°F or 4°C electrolyte temperature
1.126 at 30°F or -1.5°C electrolyte temperature

Fig. 9.1. Measuring specific gravity of battery electrolyte

1   Battery casing   3   Hydrometer
2   Cell cover

4   Electrolyte - replenishment

1   If the battery is in a fully charged state and one of the cells
maintains a specific gravity reading which is 0.025 or more lower than
the others, and a check of each cell has been made with a voltage
meter to check for short circuits (a four to seven second test should
give a steady reading of between 1.2 to 1.8 volts), then it is likely that
electrolyte has been lost from the cell with the low reading at some
time.
2   Top-up the cell with a solution of 1 part sulphuric acid to 2.5 parts
of water. If the cell is already fully topped-up draw some electrolyte
out of it with a hydrometer.
3   When mixing the sulphuric acid and water **never add water to
sulphuric acid** - always pour the acid slowly onto the water in a glass
container. **If water is added to sulphuric acid it will explode.**
4   Continue to top-up the cell with the freshly made electrolyte and
then recharge the battery and check the hydrometer readings.

5   Battery - charging

1   In winter time when heavy demand is placed upon the battery,
such as when starting from cold, and much electrical equipment is
continually in use, it is a good idea to occasionally have the battery
fully charged from an external source at the rate of 3.5 or 4 amps.
2   Continue to charge the battery at this rate until no further rise in
specific gravity is noted over a four hour period.
3   Alternatively, a trickle charger charging at the rate of 1.5 amps can
be safely used overnight.
4   Specially rapid 'boost' charges which are claimed to restore the
power of the battery in 1 to 2 hours are most dangerous as they can
cause serious damage to the battery plates.

6   Dynamo - testing in the car

1   There can be two types of faults. The charging rate may become
low, or the output may stop completely. A low output is difficult to
detect unless an ammeter is fitted. The first symptoms are likely to be
a flat battery, but a complete failure will be shown by the ignition
warning lamp coming on. Normally the lamp goes out immediately the
engine starts to charge.
2   If, with the engine running, no charge comes from the dynamo, or
the charge is low, first check that the fan belt is in place and is not

slipping. Then check that the leads from the control box to the
dynamo are firmly attached and that one has not come loose from its
terminal.
3   If wiring has recently been disconnected, check that the leads have
not been incorrectly fitted.
4   Make sure none of the electrical equipment such as the lights or
radio, is on, and then take the leads off the dynamo terminals. Join
the terminals together with a short length of wire.
5   Attach to the centre of this length of wire the positive clip of a
0-20 volts voltmeter and run the other clip to earth on the dynamo
yoke. Start the engine and allow it to idle at approximately 1500 rev/
min. At this speed the dynamo should give a reading of about 15 volts
on the voltmeter. This speed is a fast idle: Do not run the engine
faster or the field winding may be overloaded.
6   If no reading is recorded, then check the brushes and brush
connections. If a very low reading of approximately 1 volt is observed
then the field winding may be suspect.
7   If a reading of between 4 to 6 volts is recorded it is likely that the
armature winding is at fault.
8   If a satisfactory reading is obtained, then the fault is either in the
wiring or the control box. Reconnect the two wires onto the generator.
They have different sized terminals, so cannot be muddled.
9   Take off the leads on terminals 51 and 67, the left two on the
regulator. These can be muddled, so make sure they are marked to
prevent this.
10 Again join the two leads together and repeat the same test. If again
it is successful, and there is full generator voltage, then those leads
must be alright, and the fault is in the control box or the wiring beyond.
Refit the leads and refer to Section 9.

7   Dynamo - removal and refitting

1   Disconnect the lead from the battery negative terminal.
2   Unbolt and remove the front flange of the dynamo pulley and
detach the drivebelt. Retain any belt adjustment shims.
3   Disconnect the leads from the dynamo terminals (photo).
4   Reaching round behind the engine, disconnect the air inlet ducting
from the rear of the fan cooling casing.
5   The nut which secures the fan to the extension of the dynamo
armature shaft will now be exposed and it should be unscrewed. In
order to prevent the armature turning as the nut is unscrewed, hold the
flange still at the opposite end of the dynamo using a ring spanner on
the nut and lever it against a stud (photos).
6   Release the dynamo mounting strap by unscrewing the clamp bolt.
7   Unscrew the two nuts which secure the dynamo flange to the fan
cooling casing.
8   Withdraw the dynamo at the same time holding the fan within the
casing and taking care not to let the Woodruff key (which secures the
fan to the shaft) drop into the fan casing. Should this happen, retrieve
it with a magnet.
9   As the dynamo is withdrawn, tilt it to the left and upwards to
disengage the plastic positioning dowel which locates it on the support
cradle of the engine crankcase.
10 Refit the dynamo by reversing the removal operations, but if the
drivebelt requires tensioning, refer to Chapter 2, Section 5.

8   Dynamo - overhaul

1   With the dynamo removed from the car, grip the pulley flange in
the jaws of a vice and unscrew the securing nut (Fig. 9.2 and photo).
2   Remove the pulley and Woodruff key from the armature shaft
(photo).
3   Unscrew and remove the tie-bolts and withdraw the fan end frame
and the commutator end frame (photos).
4   If the dynamo has seen considerable service, the brushes will
almost certainly require renewal.
5   If the shaft bearings are worn, they can be renewed after unbolting
the bearing retainers.
6   Examine the commutator segments. If the armature has some
burned out windings with short circuits there will be burns, and the
windings may show signs of overheating.
7   Test the resistance of the windings by checking the resistance from
segment to segment. A replacement armature may be difficult to
get, and one from a vehicle breaker may have a bad commutator, so

you may be forced to get a reconditioned one.

8 Check the resistance of the field windings, an accurate ohmmeter or Wheatstone bridge must be used. See the Specifications. If the reading is very high there is an open circuit. If the reading is below the Specification, then a short circuit is indicated. If the field windings are faulty, unless a visual inspection discloses an easily mended defect, a reconditioned unit will probably be needed. Replacement windings are unlikely to be available quickly and are difficult to fit. It should be possible to get a serviceable body complete at a breakers, and put your armature into the other body.

9 If the armature is in good condition, clean the commutator with a fuel moistened rag and note whether the segments are clearly defined and free from pitting or burned areas.

10 Scrape the dirt out of the undercut gaps of insulator between the metal segments with a narrow screwdriver.

11 If, after the commutator has been cleaned, pits and burnt spots are still present, wrap a strip of fine glass paper round the commutator. Rub the patches off. Keep moving the paper along and turning the armature so that the rubbing is spread evenly all over. Finally repolish the commutator with metal polish, then reclean the gaps.

12 In extreme cases of wear the commutator can be mounted in a lathe. With the lathe turning fast, take a very fine cut. Then polish with fine glass paper, followed by metal polish.

13 If the commutator is badly worn or has been skimmed the segments may be worn till level with the insulator in between. In this case the insulator must be undercut. This is done to a depth of 0.04 in (1 mm). The best tool is a hacksaw blade, if necessary ground down to make it thinner. The under cutting must take the full width of the insulator away, right out to the metal segments on each side (Fig. 9 3).

14 Again clean all thoroughly when finished, and ensure no rough edges are left. Any roughness will cause excessive brush wear. In all this work it must also be remembered that the commutator should be treated reasonably carefully.

15 Commence reassembly by installing to the armature, first the brush endplate, with the brushes in place, pushing them back with clean fingers against the springs to get them over the commutator (photo).

16 Now lower down the body of the dynamo over the armature. Slide

the nylon tongue that is under the small terminal on the body into the post for the larger tongue on the endplate, and also located the dowel on the body.

17 Now fit the other endplate. Again locate the dowel: These dowels are very small peenings on the body, locating with grooves in the endplate.

18 Guide the ends of the tie bolts through the holes in the endplate. Do this with the dynamo upright so that the bolts will hang vertically and find their way through the holes.

19 Fit the flat washers and the self locking nuts to the bolts.

9 Regulator unit - description and testing

1 The regulator unit is located on the left-hand side of the engine compartment and comprises a cut out, a voltage regulator and a current regulator (Fig. 9.4 and photo).

2 The purpose of the cut out is to prevent the battery discharging through the dynamo once the engine is switched off and the dynamo stops charging.

3 The two regulator relays by their combination of voltage and current control regulate the output to suit the electrical load, such as lights that might be switched on, and to suit the state of charge of the battery.

4 If the control box has a complete failure the ignition warning light will come on. If there is partial failure, unless an ammeter is fitted, there will be no warning. Undercharging may become apparent as a flat battery. Minor overcharging will give the need for frequent topping-up of the battery. Gross overcharging may blow light bulbs, and perhaps result in a smell of burning, from the overloaded dynamo.

5 Major defects are likely to be the burning of the points on the relays.

6 Special instruments are required to test the regulator for faults and it is recommended that such work is left to your Fiat dealer, also any resetting which may be necessary.

7.3 Dynamo terminals and leads

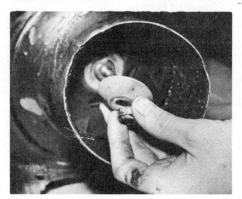
7.5a Removing the fan securing nut

7.5b Method of locking dynamo prior to removing fan securing nut

8.1 Unscrewing dynamo pulley mounting flange nut

8.2 Removing dynamo pulley mounting flange and Woodruff key

8.3a Unscrewing a dynamo tie bolt nut

8.3b Removing dynamo brush end plate

8.15 Reassembling brush end plate to dynamo armature

9.1 Location of regulator unit

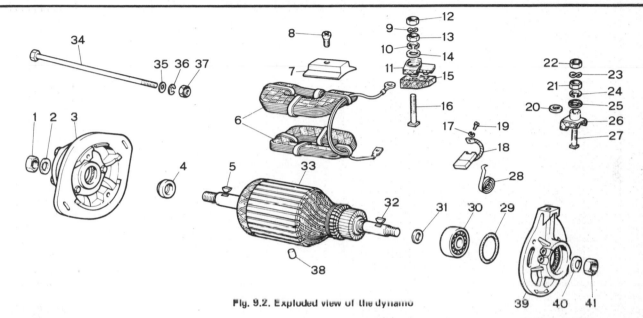

Fig. 9.2. Exploded view of the dynamo

1	Cooling fan nut	12	Terminal nut	22	Terminal nut	32	Woodruff key
2	Lockwasher	13	Terminal nut	23	Spring washer	33	Armature
3	Fan end frame	14	Plain washer	24	Lockwasher	34	Tie-bolt
4	Shouldered spacer	15	Insulator	25	Insulator	35	Plain washer
5	Woodruff key	16	Terminal	26	Insulator	36	Lockwasher
6	Field coils	17	Lockwasher	27	Terminal	37	Nut
7	Pole shoe	18	Brush	28	Brush spring	38	Locating dowel
8	Pole shoe screw	19	Brush terminal screw	29	Seal	39	Commutator end frame
9	Spring washer	20	Plain washer	30	Bearing	40	Plain washer
10	Lockwasher	21	Terminal nut	31	Plain washer	41	Pulley hub nut
11	Insulator						

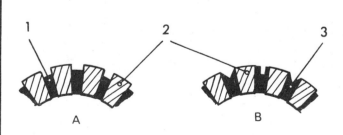

Fig. 9.3. Commutator undercutting diagram

A Correct
1 Mica insulators
2 Segments

B Incorrect
3 Mica insulators

Fig. 9.4. Regulator unit with cover removed

1	Voltage regulator contact bracket	6	Cut-out relay contact bracket
2	Voltage regulator armature	7	Connecting wire to series resistor on voltage regulator
3	Current regulator armature		
4	Cut-out relay armature	8	Current regulator contact bracket
5	Cut-out relay armature stop		

10 Starter motor - description

1   The starter is of the pre-engaged type (Fig. 9.5).
2   When the cable is pulled by the lever beside the driver an arm on the top of the starter does two things. A fork at the bottom of the actuating lever on the starter body slides the drive gear on the starter shaft towards the gear ring on the outside of the flywheel. If the teeth happen to be lined up it goes into mesh. If not lined up, the starter's gear slides on its mounting against a spring, which will push it into mesh as soon as the starter begins to turn and lines up the teeth. Once the lever has got near the end of its travel the gears are ready for the motor to turn. In the last bit of its movement the lever pushes on a switch and completes the electrical circuit.
3   Once the engine fires, the starter motor could run too fast as the engine picks up, so there is a freewheel in the drive.

11 Starter motor - removal and refitting

1   Disconnect the lead from the battery negative terminal.
2   Open the engine compartment lid and disconnect the operating cable from the switch lever on the top of the starter motor by extracting the split pin (photo).
3   Disconnect the electrical lead from the starter motor terminal.
4   Unbolt the support plate from the front end of the starter motor. This is secured under one of the driveshaft flange nuts (photo).
5   Unbolt the starter from the clutch bellhousing and lift it from the engine compartment.
6   Installation is a reversal of removal. Reconnect the operating cable to one of the three holes in the switch lever of the starter which will give the cable the minimum of slack without tending to actuate the switch lever.

12 Starter motor - overhaul

1   Remove the two Phillips headed screws that hold the starter switch to the top of the body, and take off the switch (photo and Fig. 9.6).
2   Undo the screw clamping the shield over the apertures for the brushes and remove the shield (photo).
3   Undo the two nuts on the long bolts that clamp the whole starter together, at the brush end (photo).
4   From the other end pull off the starter drive, with its engaging mechanism (photo).
5   At the windows for the brushes, undo the terminal securing the field coils in the starter body to the brush endplate. Then take off the endplate (photos).
6   To dismantle the drive mechanism, first remove the dirt shield. This is a rubber boot held by the pin of the actuating lever.
7   Remove the lever's pin (photo).

8   Push the drive pinion as far as it will go into the housing. Disconnect the forks of the engaging arm from the groove in the drive pinion, and then bring out the engaging lever fork-end first. The components of the drive can now be lifted out (photo).
9   Unscrew the switch from the top of the starter body.
10 Check the brushes for wear. It is best to renew them in any case at the time of major overhaul.
11 Clean the commutator with a fuel-soaked rag and if necessary, undercut the insulators, as described for the dynamo in Section 8.
12 Clean the bearings of the armature shaft and relubricate them after checking them for signs of wear.
13 Clean all the components of the drive, and check them for wear. Lubricate with a molybdenum - disulphide grease.
14 If any of the major components are badly worn, it may be best to get a replacement unit.
15 The bearings are self-lubricating. Place them in engine oil, allowing it time to soak in before reassembly.
16 Check the switch contacts for burning. If the starter control lever has been pulled gently too often the switch will have been burned. With gentle operation the two contacts are not firmly pressed against each other, so sparking takes place. This can lead either to the starter failing to work, or worse, not stopping when the control is released. Should the latter happen, switch off the ignition, and take off a battery lead quickly.
17 Commence reassembly with the starter drive assembly. Insert the drive pinion into the end of the housing and then engage the shift lever so that its lug is correctly located for actuating the switch.
18 Install the spring between the forks of the lever and insert the pivot pin. Make sure that the ends of the spring are holding the shift lever in the 'OFF' position.
19 Fit a new split pin into the pivot pin and then install the flexible dust excluding boot. If the boot is deformed or has deteriorated, then it should be renewed.
20 Fit the flat washer to the armature shaft at the commutator end.
21 Push the brush endplate over the commutator holding the brushes in their retracted position with the fingers.
22 Fit the body over the armature, sliding it down towards the brush-end plate with the field winding terminal lined up with its fixing in the endplate. Put the screw through the connecting tag for the brush and the terminal for the field winding, and screw it into the post on the endplate.
23 Fit the drive end. Note that the two long bolts that will hold the whole starter together are covered with insulating sleeves. As the drive unit is slid on it will be necessary to turn the drive pinion to line up the splines.
24 Put the flat washers on the ends of the long bolts, and fit the self locking nuts and tighten them.
25 Slide the dirt shield over the brush end to cover the body apertures. Fix it so that the slit at the end is not in alignment with any of the apertures.
26 Refit the switch to the top of the starter.

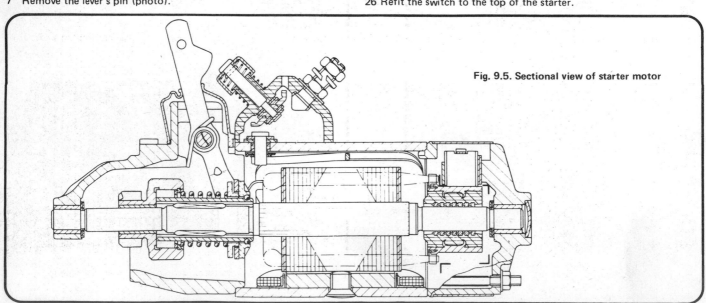

Fig. 9.5. Sectional view of starter motor

Fig. 9.6. Exploded view of the starter motor

1	Rubber boot	10	Lockwasher
2	Shift lever spring	11	Plain washer
3	Pivot pin	12	Pole shoe screw
4	Split pin	13	Pole shoe
5	Shift lever	14	Field coils
6	Switch	15	Plain washer
7	Lockwasher	16	Brush terminal screw
8	Terminal nut	17	Brush
9	Switch retaining screw		

18	Brush spring	26	Clutch sleeve
19	Commutator end frame	27	Pinion
20	Cover band screw	28	Plain washer
21	Cover band	29	Plain washer
22	Nut	30	Drive end frame
23	Bush	31	Bush
24	Plain washer	32	Tie bolt
25	Armature	33	Nut

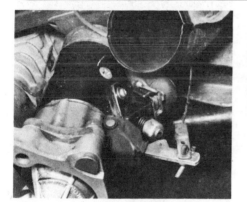

11.2 Starter switch operating cable

11.3 Starter motor front end mounting plate

12.1 Starter motor switch securing screw (arrowed)

12.2 Removing starter motor cover band

12.3 Removing starter motor tie bolt nut

12.4 Removing starter drive assembly

12.5a Disconnecting starter motor field winding terminals

12.5b Separating starter motor brush end cover from body

12.5c Removing brush end cover from starter motor armature

12.5d Extracting thrust washer from starter motor brush end cover

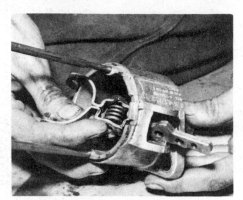

12.7 Removing starter motor shift lever and spring

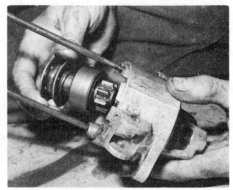

12.8 Extracting starter pinion/clutch assembly

13 Fuses - general

1　The fuses are located on a block within the luggage compartment.

2　In the event of failure of an electrical component always check the fuse to ensure that it has not blown before blaming the component (Fig. 9.7).

3　Fuses generally blow very infrequently, but may do so simultaneously when a lamp bulb fails.

4　Always renew a fuse with one of similar rating and if it blows again immediately, trace the source of the trouble instead of fitting yet another new fuse.

5　Most causes of fuses blowing are due to a breakdown in the insulation of the wiring due to age or to cutting through the cable covering on sharp edges of body or underframe. These factors will cause the cable to short circuit to earth.

14 Direction indicator flasher unit

1　The unit is located behind the instrument centre panel.

2　Remove the centre panel as described in Section 23 if access to the sealed cylindrical flasher canister is required.

3　In the event of failure of the direction indicators, first check that the connecting wiring is secure and that the bulbs (including the pilot warning) are not blown.

4　If everything is in order, renew the canister.

15 Bulbs - renewal

Headlamps

1　Access to the double filament bulbs used in the headlamps is obtained through the luggage compartment.

2　Take off the plastic shield from the back of the headlamp (photo).

3　Slide out the plug connector and remove the rubber boot from the rear of the lamp (photo).

4　Withdraw the bulb and holder by depressing the two ends of the spring ring and turning it in a clockwise direction (photo).

5　When fitting the new bulb, install the spring ring and check that the positioning dowel on the bulb aligns with the cut out on its holder.

6　If the headlamp unit is to be removed, simply pull it from the front of the car by giving it a sharp jerk to disengage its ball and socket type fixings (photo).

Front parking lamp

7　The bulb holder is pulled from the lower section of the headlamp reflector casing and the bulb extracted (photo).

Front direction indicator lamp

8　The bayonet fixing type bulb is accessible after having removed the lamp lens (two screws) (photo).

Rear lamp cluster

9　Access to the direction indicator bulb and to the double filament stop/tail bulb is obtained after removing the lens from the rear lamp cluster (three screws) (photo).

Rear number plate lamp

10　This lamp is located underneath the rear bumper. To gain access to the screws, depress the locking tabs at each end of the lamp unit and withdraw it from the lamp body.

Courtesy lamp

11　This lamp is a combined lamp and switch.

12　To renew the festoon type bulb, pull off the snap-on type lens.

Direction indicator side repeater lamps

13　These lamps are of integral construction and in the event of failure, renew the complete lamp (Fig. 9.8).

14　Disconnect the lamp leads and prise out the lamp using a screwdriver as a lever.

Instrument warning and indicator lamps

15 The lamp holders which are plugged into the back of the instrument panel are accessible from within the luggage compartment.
16 Twist the bulb holders from their locations and then extract the bulbs.
17 Refit the bulbs and push the holders into position.

16 Headlamp - beam setting

1 It is recommended that this job is carried out by your dealer, but if you wish to do the job yourself, observe the following procedure.
2 Place the car (during the hours of darkness) 16 ft (5 metres) from and square to, a wall or screen.
3 Measure the height and distance apart of the centres of the headlamps and transpose these measurements as crosses onto the wall or screen in precise alignment with the headlamp centres.
4 Switch the headlamps to dipped beam and note if the brightest points of the beams are 1.4 in (35 mm) below the crosses.
5 If this is not the case, adjust the beams by means of the adjuster screws at the back of the headlamps within the luggage boot.

17 Horn and switch

1 If the horn fails to work first check whether it is the horn button or the actual horn.
2 The horn button is a push fit in the steering wheel. If the problem is here it may be burned points due to sparking as the button makes contact.
3 The circuit from the button is to a contact by the indicator stalk on the steering column. This contact must be good. A failure here is normally given away by the horn working fitfully when the steering wheel is wiggled. The contact should be coated with petroleum jelly (Vaseline).
4 The horn button is the earth return, and is the black/yellow wire. Find which it is at the horn. Check that the other lead is live with a voltmeter or test lamp. Then earth the earth contact with an odd length of wire, to prove the horn itself is working.
5 The horn is mounted up underneath the luggage boot and in the event of it becoming faulty it must be renewed as a unit as it cannot be repaired (photo).

18 Steering column switches - removal and refitting

1 Disconnect the lead from the battery negative terminal.
2 Remove the horn button (preceding Section) at the steering wheel (Chapter 10).
3 Insert a screwdriver through the hole in the steering column shroud and release the screw which secures the direction indicator switch to the steering shaft support (Fig. 9.9).
4 Draw off the switches as required and disconnect the wiring at the multi-pin plugs.
5 Refitting is a reversal of removal, but install the steering wheel, as described in Chapter 10.

19 Windscreen wiper blades and arms - removal and refitting

1 Whenever the wiper blades fail to clean the screen effectively, renew them.
2 To do this, pull the arm away from the glass until it locks.
3 Pull the small tag to release the peg which secures the blade to the wiper arm and slide the blade off the arm (photo).
4 Install the new blade by pushing it onto the arm until the securing peg locks in the hole in the wiper blade carrier. Push the arm/blade assembly into contact with the windscreen glass.
5 To remove a wiper arm, pull the blade/arm assembly fully away from the screen until it locks and then pull the arm from the splines of the driving spindle. If any difficulty is encountered, use a small screwdriver to lever it off (photo).
6 When refitting the arm, do not push it fully home on the splines until the position of the blades on the screen has been checked. They should lie parallel with the bottom of the windscreen when the wiper motor is on the 'OFF' (parked) position.

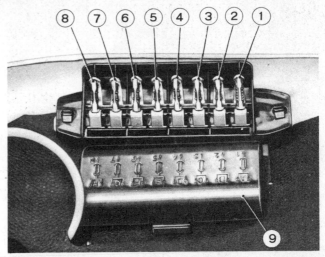

Fig. 9.7. Fuse block with cover (9) removed

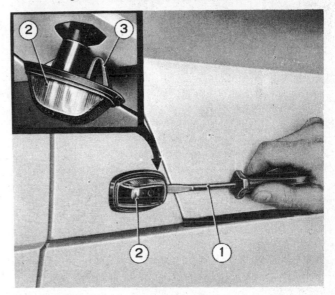

Fig. 9.8. Direction indicator side repeater lamp

1 Screwdriver 3 Snap fastener
2 Lamp assembly

Fig. 9.9. Releasing the direction indicator switch

1 Steering shaft 3 Switch securing screw
2 Direction indicator switch

15.2 Removing headlamp rear cover

15.3 Removing rubber boot from rear of headlamp

15.4 Removing headlamp bulb and holder

15.6 Removing headlamp unit from front of car

15.7 Removing front parking lamp and holder from headlamp

15.8 Front direction indicator lamp

15.9 Rear lamp cluster

15.10 Rear number plate lamp bulb holder

17.5 Location of horn

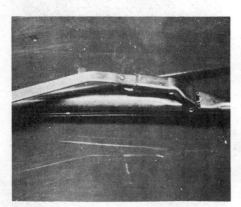
19.3 Windscreen wiper blade attachment

19.5 Removing a windscreen wiper arm

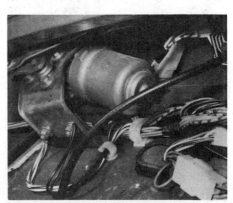
20.1 Location of windscreen wiper motor and linkage

20 Windscreen wiper motor and linkage - removal and refitting

1   The windscreen wiper motor and linkage is accessible within the luggage compartment after the covering panel has been pulled away (photo).
2   First remove the wiper blades and arms, as described in the preceding Section.
3   Unscrew and remove the securing nuts, flanges and seals which hold the driving spindles in position.
4   Unbolt the wiper motor support bracket from the body and then withdraw the complete motor linkage from the rear bulkhead of the luggage compartment far enough to be able to disconnect the electrical harness.
5   The crankarm can be unbolted from the motor and the linkage dismantled if new components are required. A faulty motor should be renewed as it is unlikely that the individual components to repair it can be obtained.
6   Installation is a reversal of removal.

21 Speedometer cable - renewal

1   Open the luggage compartment lid and withdraw the cover panel from the rear of the compartment.
2   Unscrew the knurled ring which secures the speedometer cable to the back of the speedometer (photo).
3   Normally, the inner cable can now be extracted but if it has broken, the cable assembly may have to be detached from the extension housing of the gearbox and the inner cable lower section which has broken off, pulled out from the bottom of the conduit.
4   When installing a new inner cable, apply a smear of grease to the lower two thirds of its length before pushing it into its conduit.
5   If a complete cable assembly has been installed, make sure that it follows the same route as the original with no sharp bends.

22 Instruments - removal and installation

1   Working within the luggage compartment, disconnect the speedometer cable and the electrical connectors from the back of the instruments.
2   Extract the two screws from the front face of the instrument panel and withdraw the panel (Fig. 9.10).
3   Individual instruments and lamps can then be removed from the panel (Fig. 9.11).
4   Installation is a reversal of removal.

23 Centre panel - removal and installation

1   Extract the two screws which secure the panel (Fig. 9.12).
2   Pull the panel far enough towards you to be able to disconnect the washer hoses from the washer pump and the connector plug from the back of the lighting switch. Remove the panel.
3   Installation is a reversal of removal.

24 Windscreen washer assembly

1   A manually-operated washer assembly is fitted and comprises, a curiously shaped fluid reservoir within the luggage compartment, a pump mounted on the centre panel of the fascia and the necessary pipes and jets (Fig. 9.13).
2   The stream of washer fluid ejected from the jets should strike the screen at the top of the glass which is swept by the wiper blades. Adjust if necessary with a screwdriver.
3   Keep the interior of the fluid bag clean and if the jets become blocked, they can be cleaned with a pin.
4   Periodically clean the filter screen of the reservoir pick-up tube with a stiff brush.
5   Always use solvent in the washer reservoir water and in cold weather add methylated spirit to prevent it freezing.

Fig. 9.10. Instrument panel securing screws

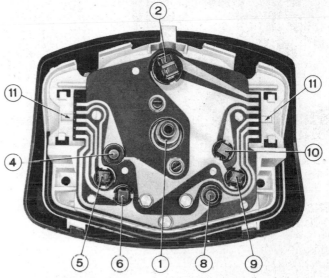

Fig. 9.11. Reverse side of instrument panel

1   Speedometer
2   Parking lamp indicator lamp
4   Spare position for indicator lamp
5   Ignition warning lamp
6   Oil pressure warning lamp
8   Low fuel level lamp (Nov 1974 onwards)
9   Main beam warning lamp
10   Direction indicator warning lamp
11   Circuit connections

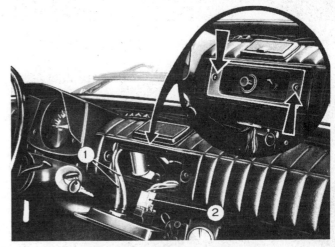

Fig. 9.12. Centre panel removal

1   Washer hoses
2   Lighting switch multi-pin connector
3   Flasher unit

2.1 Rear view of instrument panel

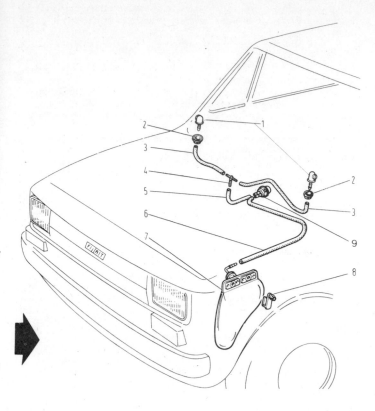

Fig. 9.13. Windscreen washer components

1 Jet nozzle
2 Bush
3 Hose
4 Three-way connector
5 Hose
6 Hose
7 Fluid reservoir
8 Reservoir securing hook
9 Pump

25 Fault diagnosis - electrical system

Symptom	Reason/s
Starter motor fails to turn engine No electricity at starter motor	Battery discharged. Battery defective internally. Battery terminal leads loose or earth lead not securely attached to body. Loose or broken connections in starter motor circuit. Starter motor switch faulty.
Electricity at starter motor: faulty motor	Starter motor pinion jammed in mesh with flywheel gear ring. Starter brushes badly worn, sticking, or brush wires loose. Commutator dirty, worn or burnt. Starter motor armature faulty. Field coils earthed.
Starter motor turns engine very slowly Electrical defects	Battery in discharged condition. Starter brushes badly worn, sticking, or brush wires loose. Loose wires in starter motor circuit.
Starter motor operates without turning engine Mechanical damage	Pinion or flywheel gear teeth broken or worn.
Starter motor noisy or excessively rough engagement Lack of attention or mechanical damage	Pinion or flywheel gear teeth broken or worn. Starter motor retaining bolts loose.
Battery will not hold charge for more than a few days Wear or damage	Battery defective internally. Electrolyte level too low or electrolyte too weak due to leakage. Plate separators no longer fully effective. Battery plates severely sulphated.

Insufficient current flow to keep battery charged

Battery plates severely sulphated.
Fanbelt slipping.
Battery terminal connections loose or corroded.
Dynamo not charging.
Short in lighting circuit causing continual battery drain.
Regulator unit not working correctly.

Ignition light fails to go out, battery runs flat in a few days
Dynamo not charging

Fanbelt loose and slipping or broken.
Brushes worn, sticking, broken or dirty.
Brush springs weak or broken.
Commutator dirty, greasy, worn or burnt.
Dynamo field coils burnt, open, or shorted.
Commutator worn.
Pole pieces very loose.

Regulator or cut-out fails to work correctly

Regulator incorrectly set.
Cut-out incorrectly set.
Open circuit in wiring of cut-out and regulator unit.

Horn
Horn operates all the time

Horn push either earthed or stuck down.

Horn fails to operate

Blown fuse.
Cable or cable connection loose, broken or disconnected.
Horn has an internal fault.

Horn emits intermittent or unsatisfactory noise

Cable connections loose.
Horn incorrectly adjusted.

Lights
Lights do not come on

If engine not running, battery discharged.
Lamp bulbs broken.
Wire connections loose, disconnected or broken.
Light switch shorting or otherwise faulty.

Lights come on but fade out

If engine not running battery discharged.
Light bulb filament burnt out.
Wire connections loose, disconnected or broken.
Light switch shorting or otherwise faulty.

Lights give very poor illumination

Lamp glasses dirty.
Lamp badly out of adjustment.

Lights work erratically - flashing on and off, especially over bumps

Battery terminals or earth connection loose.
Light not earthing properly.
Contacts in light switch faulty.

Wipers
Wiper motor fails to work

Blown fuse.
Wire connections loose, disconnected, or broken.
Brushes badly worn.
Armature worn or faulty.
Field coils faulty.

Wiper motor works very slowly and takes excessive current

Commutator dirty, greasy or burnt.
Armature bearings dirty or unaligned.
Armature badly worn or faulty.

Wiper motor works slowly and takes little current

Brushes badly worn.
Commutator dirty, greasy or burnt.
Armature badly worn or fault,

Wiper motor works but wiper blades remain static

Wiper motor gearbox parts badly worn.

Wipers do not stop when switched off or stop in wrong place

Auto-stop device faulty.

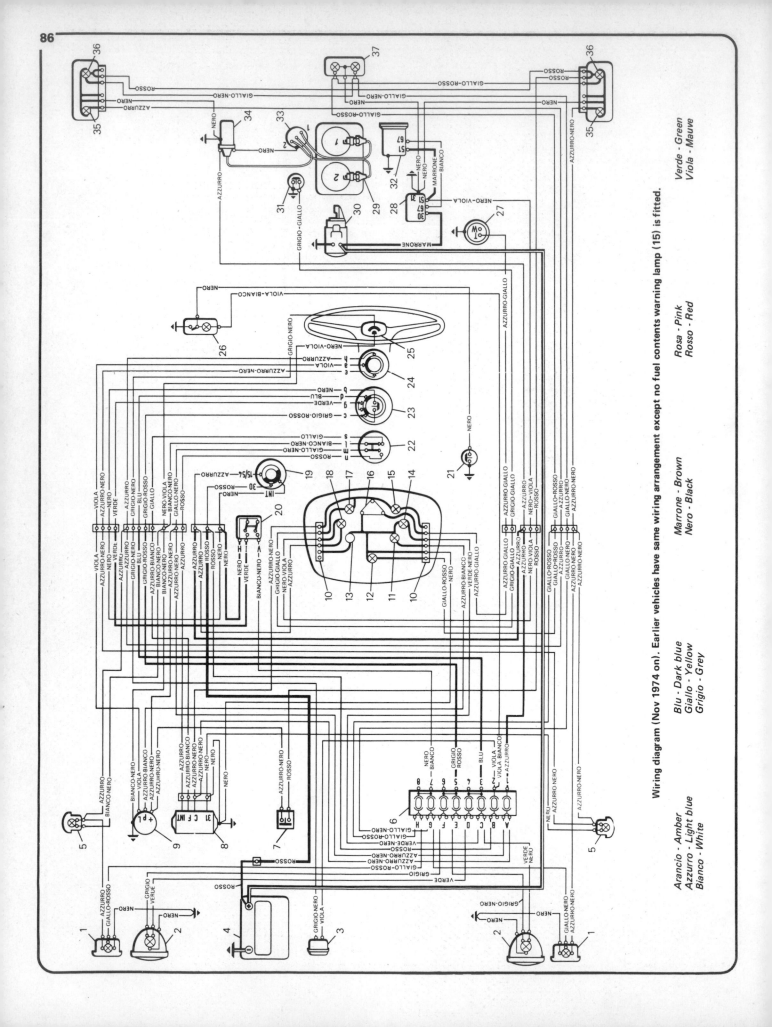

Wiring diagram (Nov 1974 on). Earlier vehicles have same wiring arrangement except no fuel contents warning lamp (15) is fitted.

Arancio - Amber
Azzurro - Light blue
Bianco - White

Blu - Dark blue
Giallo - Yellow
Grigio - Grey

Marrone - Brown
Nero - Black

Rosa - Pink
Rosso - Red

Verde - Green
Viola - Mauve

Key to Wiring Diagram

1 Front parking and turn signal lights
2 High/low beam headlights
3 Horn
4 Battery
5 Turn signal side repeaters
6 Protection fuses
7 Stop light press switch
8 Windshield wiper motor
9 Turn signal flasher
10 Junctions in instrument cluster
11 Turn signal indicator (green)
12 Parking light indicator (green) and instrument cluster light
13 Spare indicator
14 High beam indicator (blue)
15 Fuel warning light (red) [Starting from chassis N. 4231505 onward]
16 Fuel gauge
17 Low oil pressure warning light (red)
18 No-charge warning light (red)
19 Ignition and starting key switch

20 Exterior lighting switch
21 Courtesy light press switch, on driver's side door pillar
22 Windshield wiper lever switch
23 High/low beam change-over switch and signal flasher
24 Turn signal switch
25 Horn button
26 Courtesy light with built-in switch, above rear view mirror
27 Fuel gauge sending unit
28 Generator regulator unit
29 Spark plugs
30 Starting motor
31 Low oil pressure sending unit
32 Generator
33 Ignition distributor
34 Ignition coil
35 Rear turn signal lights
36 Tail and stop lights
37 License plate lights

Chapter 10 Suspension and steering

Contents

Specifications

Front suspension

Type	Independent with transverse leaf spring and telescopic shock absorbers
Number of spring leaves	5
Front hub bearing endfloat	0.001 to 0.004 in (0.025 to 0.10 mm)
Camber *	0° 30' to 1° 30' positive
Castor *	8° to 10° positive
Steering axis inclination	6° positive
Toe-in *	0 to 0.12 in (0 to 3 mm)

* Set with car loaded with equivalent of four people

Rear suspension

Type	Independent with triangular shaped control arms, coil springs and telescopic shock absorbers

Spring identification **

Yellow	Height 6.22 in (158 mm) under load of 875 lb (397 kg)
Green	Height greater than 6.22 in (158 mm) under a load of 875 lb (397 kg)

* * Rear coil springs must always be fitted in pairs with the same colour coding

Camber (non-adjustable):	
Up to 1974	0° 20' to 1° 20' negative
1974 on	0° 22' to 1° 22' negative
Toe-in	0.197 to 0.354 in (5 to 9 mm)

Steering

Type	Worm and sector with three section universally-jointed shaft
Ratio	13 : 1
Turning circle	28 ft 2 in (8.6 m)
Number of steering wheel turns (lock-to-lock)	3
Steering lock anges:	
Inner wheel	33°
Outer wheel	25° 40'
Oil capacity	4.2 fluid oz (0.12 litres)

Wheels and tyres

Wheels	Pressed steel 4.00 x 12 in
Tyres	Radial ply 135 - 12
Pressures:	
Front	20 lb/sq in (1.4 kg/sq cm)
Rear	28 lb/sq in (1.97 kg/sq cm)

Torque wrench settings

	lb f ft	Nm
Front suspension		
Roadwheel bolt	36	50
Leaf spring eye pivot bolt	29	40
Upper control arm inner pivot nut	18	25
Upper control arm pivot to bodyframe	22	30
Leaf spring clamp to body nuts	22	30
Upper control arm outer pivot bolt	44	61
Shock absorber mounting nuts	15	21
Brake backplate nuts	15	21
Rear suspension		
Roadwheel bolt	36	50
Control arm to bodyframe bolts	36	50
Control arm pivot bolt	58	65
Shock absorber mounting nuts	22	30
Brake drum bolts	60	83
Brake backplate to control arm	40	55
Steering		
Steering wheel nut	36	50
Steering column shaft pinch bolt	18	25
Steering column support bracket nuts	11	15
Steering box mounting nuts	22	30
Drop arm nut	72	100
Idler assembly mounting nuts	22	30
Idler arm nut	50	69
Trackrod clamp pinch bolt	11	15
Balljoint taper pin nuts	25	35

1 General description

1 *The front suspension* is of independent type having a transverse leaf spring and upper wishbones (Fig. 10.1).
2 The spring is attached to the bodyframe and also serves as a stabiliser bar.
3 Telescopic type shock absorbers are fitted.
4 *The rear suspension* is also of independent type but comprises semi-trailing arms and coil springs (Fig. 10.2).
5 Telescopic shock absorbers are also fitted at the rear, inside the spring coils.
6 *The steering gear* is of worm and sector type with a three section universally jointed steering column (Fig. 10.3).
7 *Roadwheels* are of pressed steel type having 4 in (102 mm) rims and are fitted with radial ply tyres.

2 Maintenance and inspection

1 At the intervals recommended in 'Routine Maintenance' apply the grease gun to the nipples on the stub axle carriers.
2 At the specified intervals, check the oil level in the steering box after having removed the side plug.
3 At the specified intervals, check the front wheel bearing adjustment and repack them with fresh grease, as described in Section 4.
4 The safety of the vehicle depends more on the steering and suspension than anything else and regular inspection of these components should be carried out.
5 Have an assistant lift the rear of the vehicle body up and down and check any movement in the top and bottom rear shock absorber mountings. Renew the bushes as necessary.
6 Also check for movement in the transverse spring bushes and eyes and for a broken or cracked spring leaf and renew as described later in this Chapter.
7 Any signs of oil on the outside of the rear shock absorber bodies will indicate that the seals have started to leak and the units must be renewed as assemblies. Where the shock absorber has failed internally, this is more difficult to detect. When a shock absorber is suspected to have failed, remove it from the vehicle and holding it in a vertical position operate it for the full length of its stroke eight or ten times. Any lack of resistance in either direction will indicate the need for renewal.
8 Any movement of the steering wheel which is not followed by corresponding movement of the front roadwheels will indicate one of

the following:

a) *Wear in the steering box internal components.*
b) *Wear in the steering linkage balljoints.*
c) *Slackness or wear in the steering column universal joints or splines or slack pinch bolts.*

9 Regularly check the balljoint flexible boots for splits or deterioration and renew as necessary.
10 Periodically check the torque wrench settings of all suspension and steering nuts and bolts.
11 Wear in the front suspension stub axle carrier bushes or any of the suspension flexible bushes can be detected if an assistant rocks the car or roadwheels and the movement of adjacent components in relation to each other is observed.

3 Shock absorbers and rear coil spring - removal and installation

1 *To remove a front shock absorber,* raise the car on a jack and remove the roadwheel.
2 The suspension should now be compressed before disconnecting the upper mounting of the shock absorber. To do this, either have an assistant push down on the top of the front wing or place a second jack under the stub axle carrier and raise the jack until the transverse leaf spring takes on a horizontal appearance at the end being worked on.
3 Working within the luggage boot, hold the flats on the top of the shock absorber spindle still, while the locknut is unscrewed (Fig. 10.4).
4 Remove the upper mounting components and then contract the shock absorber to release it from the wing inner valance.
5 Disconnect the shock absorber lower mounting in a similar way and withdraw it from under the wing (Fig. 10.5).
6 *To remove a rear shock absorber,* first lift the front of the rear seat cushion to disengage it from its locating dowels. Withdraw the seat cushion forward to expose the shock absorber upper mountings (Fig. 10.6).
7 Place a jack under the suspension arm and raise it until the roadwheel leaves the ground. Now sit in the rear seat cushion pan as close as possible to the shock absorber mounting which will have the effect of compressing the rear suspension coil spring.
8 Hold the flats on the shock absorber spindle quite still with one spanner while the locknut is released.
9 Climb out of the car; as your weight in removed, the shock absorber

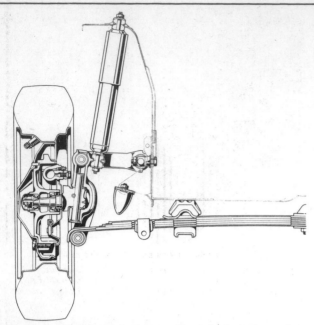

Fig. 10.1. Cross sectional view of one side of the front suspension

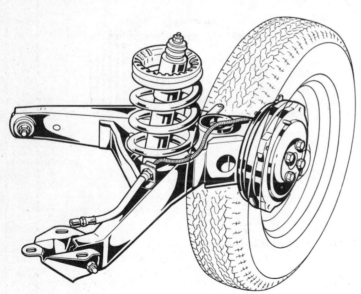

Fig. 10.2. Rear suspension layout (one side)

will detach itself from the bodyframe. Retain the upper mounting components in order.

10 With the rear suspension fully extended, the coil spring can be withdrawn and the shock absorber lower mounting disconnected and the shock absorber removed from the car (Fig. 10.7).

11 Installation of the front and rear shock absorbers is a reversal of the removal operations, but make sure that the spindle is held still while the locknut is tightened to the specified torque wrench setting.

4 Front hubs - overhaul and adjustment

1   Jack-up the front of the car and remove the roadwheel.

2   Tap off the grease cap from the end of the stub axle.

3   Relieve the staking on the nut and unscrew and remove it together with the thrust washer (photo). The right-hand nut has a left-hand thread.

4   Pull the brake drum towards you and catch the outer taper roller bearing. Remove the brake drum.

5   Provided the bearings are in good condition and the oil seal shows no sign of seepage, clean away all the old grease and repack the bearings and hub interior with fresh multi-purpose lubricant.

6   The brake drum and hub can now be refitted.

7   If the bearings are worn or the oil seal is leaking, then the components will have to be renewed.

8   If only the oil seal is to be renewed, it can be extracted by levering it from its seat and a new one tapped squarely into position (photo).

9   If the outer bearing is to be renewed, draw out the bearing track from the centre of the brake drum and then press or drive in the new one squarely.

10 If the inner tapered roller bearing is to be renewed, then it will mean destroying the oil seal in order to extract the bearing and tracks.

11 If the bearings are worn, never attempt to renew just the races leaving the old tracks in position. If both front wheels are being dismantled at the same time, never mix the new bearing races and tracks but keep them in their boxes until required. The bearing components are matched in production and are not interchangeable.

12 Install the reassembled drum/hub, well packed with grease, fit the outer bearing race and the thrust washer.

13 Screw on a new nut to a torque wrench setting of 5lb f ft (7 Nm). Where a torque wrench covering this range is not available, tighten the nut as hard as you can gripping it with the hands only. Now unscrew the nut through 30° which will give the correct endfloat of the drum/hub of between 0.001 and 0.004 in (0.025 and 0.100 mm). This can be measured using a dial gauge or feeler blades.

14 When the adjustment is correct, stake the nut into the cut out in the end of the stub axle using a narrow punch. Take care not to damage the threads on the stub axle. Remember that the right-hand nut has a left-hand thread.

15 Refit the grease cap, the roadwheel and lower the car to the ground.

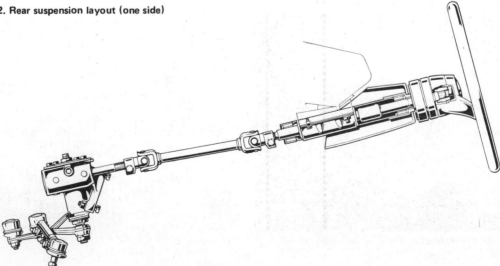

Fig. 10.3. Steering column and box

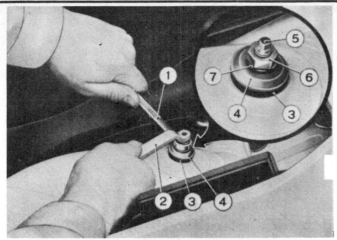

Fig. 10.4. Front shock absorber upper mounting

1 Spanner	5 Shock absorber spindle
2 Spanner	6 Locknut
3 Rubber bush	7 Lockwasher
4 Cup	

Fig. 10.5. Front shock absorber lower mounting

1 Shock absorber spindle	6 Rubber cushion
2 Suspension upper control arm	7 Cup
3 Steering arm	8 Flat washer
4 Stub axle carrier	9 Locknut and lockwasher
5 Cups	10 Lower cushion

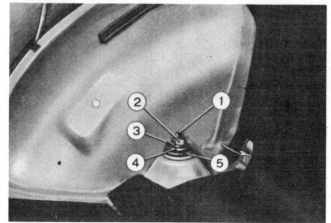

Fig. 10.6. Rear shock absorber upper mounting

1 Shock absorber spindle	4 Plain washer
2 Locknut	5 Rubber cushion
3 Lockwasher	

Fig. 10.7. Rear shock absorber lower mounting

1 Suspension control arm	4 Locknut
2 Coil spring	5 Plain washer
3 Shock absorber spindle	6 Rubber cushion

4.3 Staking of front stub axle nut

4.8 Front brake drum showing oil seal

5 Rear hubs - overhaul and adjustment

1   These operations are described in Chapter 7, Section 4, as part of the driveshaft assemblies.

6 Front leaf spring - removal, overhaul and refitting

1   Jack-up the front of the car and support it securely under the body-frame side members.
2   Place a jack under one end of the leaf spring and take its weight off the stub axle carrier.
3   Unscrew the pivot bolt from the spring eye and disconnect the spring from the stub axle carrier (Fig. 10.8).
4   Lower the jack gently from under the spring and repeat the operations at the opposite end of the spring.
5   Release the clamps which secure the spring to the bodyframe and remove the spring from the car.
6   Clean the spring leaves and examine for cracks. If any are found, the complete spring must be renewed as individual leaves are not supplied.
7   Examine the flexible bushes. If these appear to have deteriorated or if their centre sleeves are no longer central or have worn oval, then the bushes should be pressed out of the spring eyes and new ones installed. If a press is not available, remove the bushes with a long bolt, nuts, washers and suitable tubular distance pieces.
8   Check the condition of the spring to bodyframe clamp and rebound stops. Renew if necessary.
9   Install the spring by reversing the removal method using a jack to apply leverage to the spring eye.

7 King pins and bushes - renewal

1   The stub axle and king pin housing assembly can be removed quite simply.
2   Jack-up the front of the car. Transfer the weight to blocks under the body, spreading the weight broadly, and making sure that the car is very secure.
3   Move the jack to the outer end of the spring, and take some of the weight on this, so that the shock absorber is telescoped.
4   Remove the roadwheel, brake drum/hub and the brake backplate. This is held by one nut on a stud through the steering arm, and another to the rear of the king pin. Lift off the backplate, still with the brake shoes on it, and the hydraulic pipe connected. Take care the hydraulic pipe is not strained by pulling or twisting. Tie the backplate up out of the way, or prop it up.
5   Disconnect the balljoint taper pin of the trackrod-end from the steering arm.
6   Disconnect the shock absorber lower mounting from the suspension control arm
7   Telescope the shock absorber as far as it will go and take off the lower mounting components.
8   Remove the nut from the pivot bolt through the spring eye at the bottom of the king pin housing. Drive out the bolt (Fig. 10.9 and photo).
9   Lower the jack under the spring. Pull the king pin housing clear of the spring, so that it is hanging from the wishbone at the top.
10 Repeat for the bolt through the top of the king pin housing and the wishbone. Now pull the whole king pin housing and stub axle assembly away.
11 Note all the washers, and where they came from.
12 The king pin is pegged to the stub axle carrier. To remove it hammer out the pin with a punch. Prise out the disc peened into the bottom of the stub axle carrier closing the bottom bush.
13 Press out the rubber bush from the top of the stub axle carrier. Drive out the king pin from above through the space vacated by the rubber bush. If the disc at the bottom could not be removed, provided it has been loosened, it can be driven out with the king pin.
14 As the king pin comes out of its housing and the stub axle carrier is removed, note the position of all the washers. There is a load carrying washer and rubber dirt seal above. Below is a spacer.
15 The king pin replacement kit should include a pin for locking the stub axle carrier to the king pin, and all the washers and seals needed but there are many different thicknesses of spacers; but the original ones should not need changing.
16 Take the old bushes out of the housing. If difficulty is found in pressing them out they can be collapsed by cutting with a hack saw downwards to split them.
17 Press in the new bushes.
18 The bushes must now be in-line reamed to an internal diameter of between 0.5911 to 0.5922 in (15.016 to 15.043 mm). If a suitable reamer is not available, have your Fiat dealer do this for you.
19 For reassembly, grease the king pin and bushes. Get the stub axle into place in the carrier. Put all the washers in place, holding them with grease.
20 Fit the new king pin, lining up its groove with the hole in the stub axle for the locking pin.
21 Hammer in the locking pin firmly. Fit the disc to the bottom bush, and peen it into place, being careful not to damage the disc.
22 Reassemble by reversing the dismantling operations but do not fully tighten the pivot bolts at the top and bottom of the stub axle carrier until the weight of the car is again on the roadwheels. This will prevent distortion of the flexible bushes.
23 Always check the front wheel alignment after major overhaul of the front suspension (see Section 17).

Fig. 10.8. The front suspension

1 Shock absorber lower mounting	3 Shock absorber lower mounting	5 Stub axle carrier 8 Stub axle carrier
2 Rebound stops	4 Leaf spring eye pivot	6 Leaf spring clamps 9 Spring eye pivot bolt
		7 Spring

Fig. 10.9. Exploded view of one side of the front suspension

1 Locknut
2 Lockwasher
3 Cup
4 Rubber cushion
5 Rubber cushion
6 Shock absorber
7 Nut
8 Cup
9 Rubber bush
10 Spacer
11 Pivot shaft
12 Adjustment shim
(castor and camber angles)
13 Spacer
14 Control arm sections
15 Nut
16 Lockwasher
17 Plain washer
18 Rubber cushion
19 Cup
20 Leaf spring
21 Cup
22 Rubber cushion
23 Plain washer
24 Lockwasher
25 Locknut
26 Pivot nut
27 Stub axle carrier
28 Plug
29 King pin bushes
30 Pivot bolt
31 Upper control arm
pivot nut
32 Lockwasher
33 Flexible bush
34 Pivot bolt

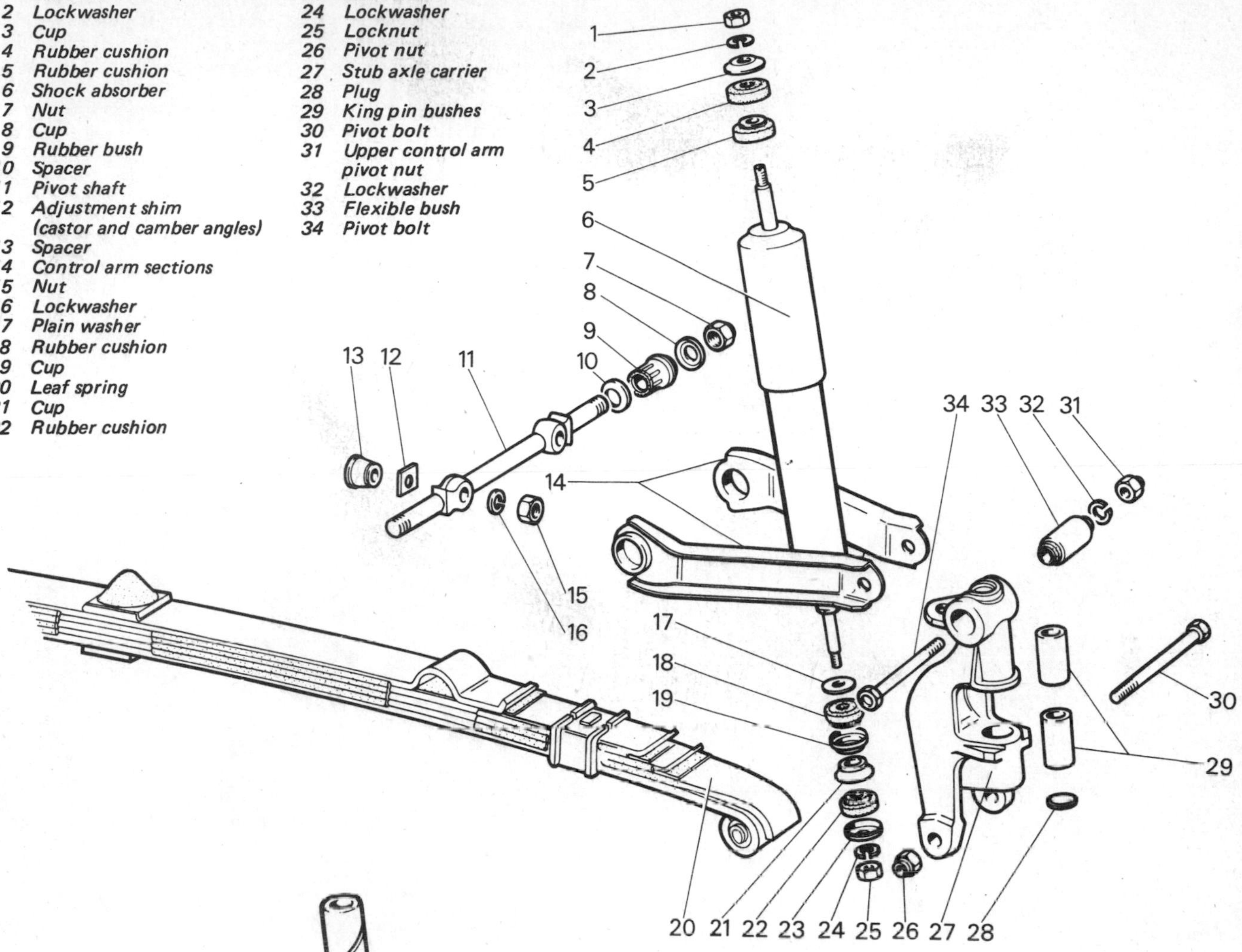

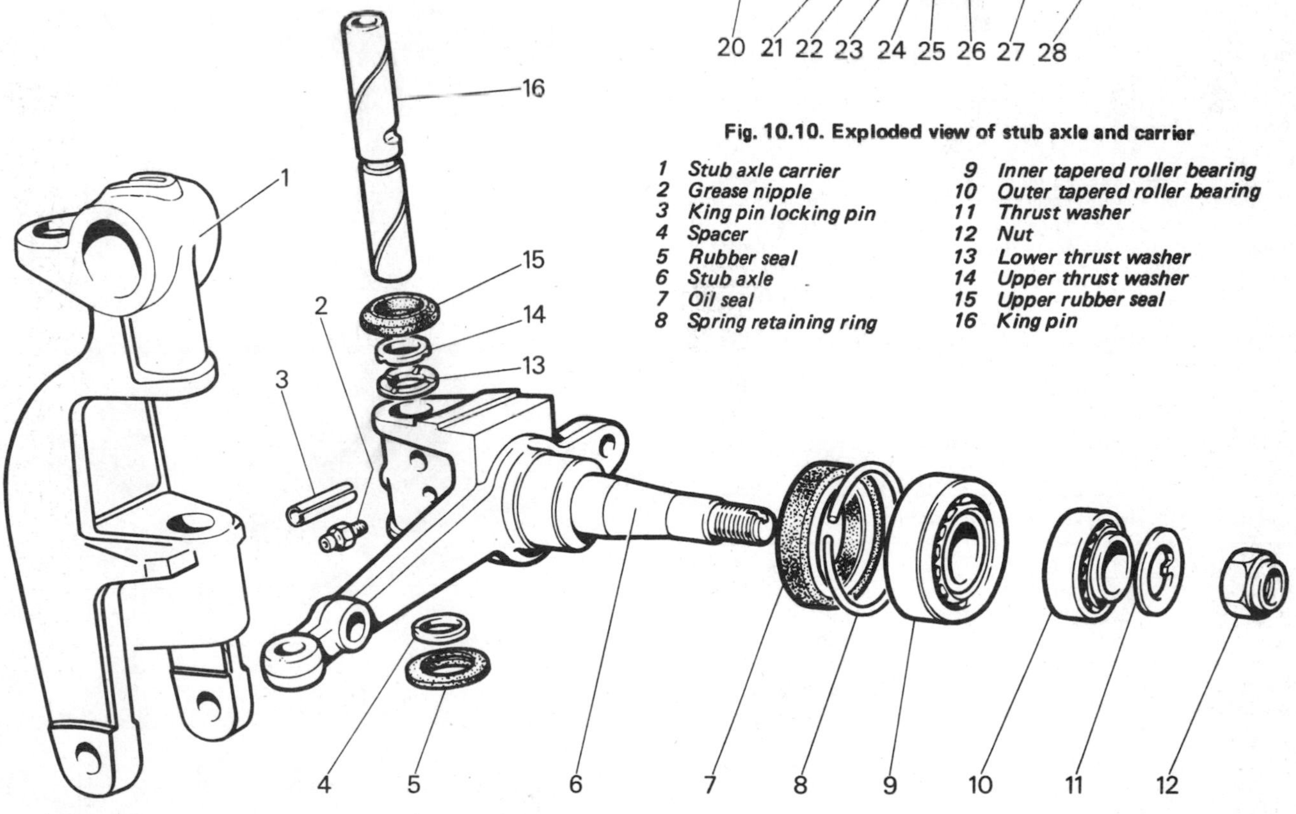

Fig. 10.10. Exploded view of stub axle and carrier

1 Stub axle carrier
2 Grease nipple
3 King pin locking pin
4 Spacer
5 Rubber seal
6 Stub axle
7 Oil seal
8 Spring retaining ring
9 Inner tapered roller bearing
10 Outer tapered roller bearing
11 Thrust washer
12 Nut
13 Lower thrust washer
14 Upper thrust washer
15 Upper rubber seal
16 King pin

Fig. 10.11. Reaming king pin bushes

1   Reamer holder   3   Stub axle carrier
2   Reamer

7.8 One side of the front suspension

8   Front suspension upper control arm bushes - renewal

1   Jack-up the front of the car, remove the roadwheel and disconnect the shock absorber lower mounting, while keeping the underside of the leaf spring eye supported on a second jack.
2   Support the brake drum in the vertical attitude and unscrew and remove the pivot bolt which secures the outer end of the control arm to the top of the stub axle carrier.
3   Remove the nuts which secure the control arm inner pivot shaft to the bodyframe.
4   Withdraw the control arm but identify in respect of location and retain the shims which are fitted on the studs behind the pivot shafts. These shims control the castor and camber angles.
5   Renew the bushes in the control arm with a press or by using a bolt, washers and distance pieces to draw them out and to refit them. Renew the bush at the top of the stub axle carrier in the same way.
6   Reassembly is a reversal of removal and dismantling.

9   Front suspension - removal, overhaul and installation

1   When all the king pin bushes have to be renewed or the upper track control arm bushes require attention, it is recommended that the complete front suspension is removed as an assembly. This will be just as quick and provide better access than removing individual suspension components.
2   Jack-up the front of the car and support it securely on axle stands placed under the bodyframe side members.
3   Remove the roadwheels.
4   Disconnect the trackrod-end balljoints from the steering arms of the stub axles. A ball joint taper pin separator will be required for this, or forked wedges (Fig. 10.12).
5   Disconnect the shock absorber upper mountings (see Section 3) and then the lower mountings.

6   Unscrew the nuts which secure the suspension control arm pivot shafts to the bodyframe. Slide the control arms from the studs, taking great care to identify and retain the shims which are located on the studs behind the pivot shafts. These shims control the castor and camber angles (Fig. 10.13).
7   Disconnect the brake hydraulic hoses at the support brackets and plug or cap the hose ends to prevent loss of fluid or the entry of dirt (photo).
8   Support the centre of the transverse leaf spring on a trolley jack and then disconnect the spring clamps from the bodyframe.
9   Remove the front suspension complete from under the car (Fig. 10.14).
10 Dismantle the upper control arm by withdrawing both pivot shafts.
11 Disconnect the stub axle carrier from the leaf spring by removing the spring eye pivot bolt.
12 Remove the drum/hub components, as described in Section 4.
13 Service the king pin bushes, as described in Section 7.
14 Service the control arm bushes, as described in Section 8.
15 Reassembly and installation are reversals of removal and dismantling, but make sure that the shims which control camber and castor are returned to their original locations and bleed the front brake hydraulic circuit on completion.

9.7 Front brake hose attachment

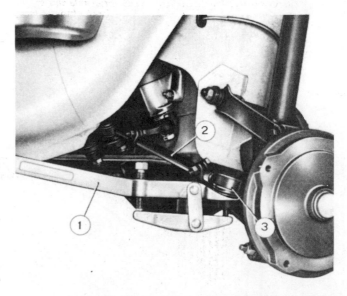

Fig. 10.12. Disconnecting a track rod balljoint

1   Extractor   3   Balljoint
2   Trackrod

10 Rear suspension - removal, overhaul and installation

1 Raise the rear of the car and support securely under the bodyframe members. Remove the roadwheels.

2 Disconnect the shock absorber upper mountings, as described in Section 3, having a second jack under the suspension control arm.

3 Disconnect the driveshaft outer coupling from the flexible joint of the axle stub.

4 Push the coupling aside and extract the small coil spring from its open end (Fig. 10.15).

5 Disconnect the brake hydraulic flexible hose at the attachment bracket on the control arm. Plug or cap the hose and pipe to prevent loss of fluid (Fig. 10.16).

6 Disconnect the handbrake cable from the lever on the brake backplate.

7 Lower the jack under the control arm, compress the shock absorber and slide out the coil spring with its two rubber insulators.

8 Before unscrewing the bolts which secure the suspension control arm bracket to the bodyframe, mark the exact position of the bracket on the bodyframe. This can either be done by marking round the edge of the bracket or by giving a quick spray with paint from an aerosol. This will leave the position of the bracket clearly defined on the bodyframe once it has been removed (Fig. 10.17).

9 Unbolt the control arm bracket from the bodyframe.

10 Unscrew and remove the pivot bolt which secures the inner section of the control arm to the bodyframe. Take care to identify and retain any shims which are located either side of the flexible bushes at this attachment point (Fig. 10.18).

11 Withdraw the control arm assembly complete with brake drum and axle stub (Fig. 10.19).

12 The control arm flexible bushes can be renewed by extracting and installing them with a press or by using a bolt and nut, washers and suitable distance pieces.

13 Dismantling of the axle stub and hub bearings is described in Chapter 7, Section 4.

14 Repeat the foregoing operations on the opposite suspensions assembly if required.

15 Reassembly and installation are reversals of removal and dismantling. Make sure that the control arm support bracket is refitted in exactly its previously marked position, also the shims are returned to their original positions on the inner control arm pivot. Failure to observe either of these points will upset the rear wheel alignment.

16 Tighten the control arm pivot and bracket bolts to the specified torque wrench settings.

17 Bleed the brake hydraulic circuit for the rear brakes.

18 Although the rear wheel alignment should not have been altered if the suspension control arm has been attached in its original position, it

Fig. 10.13. Front suspension upper control arm detail

1 Flexible bush
2 Castor and camber adjusting shims
3 Control arm
4 Pivot shaft
5 Pivot shaft
6 Stub axle carrier
7 Shock absorber lower mounting
8 Shock absorber spindle

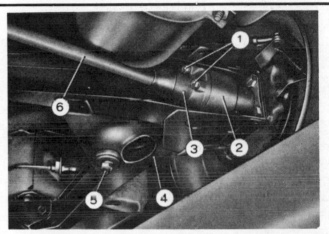

Fig. 10.15. View of right-hand rear suspension assembly

1 Driveshaft outer coupling bolts
2 Flexible joint
3 Splined sleeve
4 Suspension control arm
5 Shock absorber lower mounting
6 Driveshaft

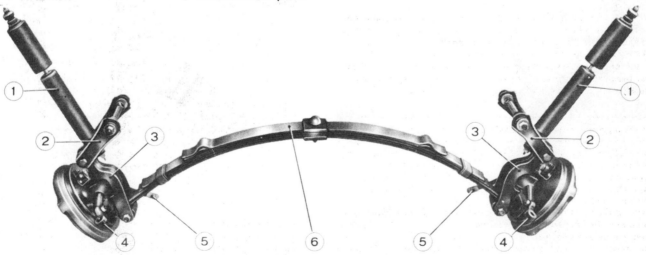

Fig. 10.14. Complete front suspension removed from car

1 Shock absorbers
2 Suspension upper control arm
3 Stub axle carriers
4 Steering arm
5 Flexible brake hoses
6 Leaf spring

Fig. 10.16. View of left-hand rear suspension assembly

1 Brake hose connection   3 Handbrake cable
2 Coil spring

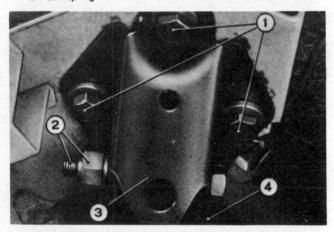

Fig. 10.17. Rear suspension attachment to bodyframe

1 Securing bolts   3 Bracket
2 Pivot bolt and nut 4 Control arm

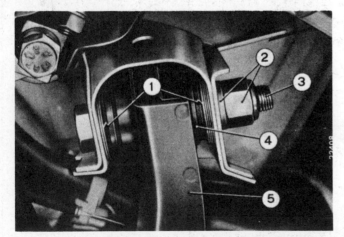

Fig. 10.18. Attachment of inner end of rear suspension control arm to bodyframe

1 Adjustment shims   4 Rubber bush
2 Nut and lockwasher   5 Control arm
3 Pivot bolt

is strongly recommended that the alignment is checked after major overhaul. Refer also to Section 19 for detailed information on the setting of the rear wheel toe-in.

11 Trackrod-end ball joints - removal and refitting

1   The steering linkage comprises a centre and two outer trackrod sections (Fig. 10.20).
2   The trackrod-end ball joint assemblies on the outer trackrods are renewable but the ones at each end of the centre rod are integral with the rod and must be renewed as a complete assembly.
3   Any wear in the ball joints must be rectified immediately by renewal of the components.
4   To disconnect a ball joint taper pin from the stub axle carrier steering arm, the idler drop arm or the steering drop arm, first unscrew the securing nut and then separate the ball joint from the eye of the arm using a ball joint extractor or forked wedges. If these tools are not available they can often be hired. Do not waste time using the old fashioned idea of hitting the eye with two club hammers as damage is likely to be done to adjacent components.
5   With the taper pin separated from the eye, in the case of the outer trackrod joints, mark the number of exposed threads so that the new ball joint assembly can be positioned in the same relative position as the original one.
6   Release the clamp pinch bolt and unscrew the trackrod-end ball joint from the track rod.
7   Grease the threads of the new balljoint assembly and screw it into the trackrod until the equivalent number of exposed threads as there were originally are showing. The outer trackrod ball joint assemblies are supplied in pairs (LH and RH) so that when installed, the hollow trackrod tube can be rotated to effectively increase or decrease the length of the rod assembly in order to vary the front wheel alignment (toe-in).
8   Locate the balljoint taper pin in the eye of the arm and tighten the nut to the specified torque. If there is a tendency for the ball joint pin to rotate as the nut is tightened, apply pressure to force it further into its seat. Do not apply grease to the taper pin when assembling as this will aggravate this problem.
9   Set the ball joint in its correct attitude at the centre of its arc of travel and then position the clamp so that its slot is in alignment with the slot in the trackrod tube. Tighten the pinch bolt.
10 Even though the greatest care may have been taken to install the new trackrod-end ball joints in the same relative position as the original ones, always have the front wheel alignment (toe-in) checked as soon as possible by your Fiat dealer or by reference to Section 17. This applies even if the centre trackrod assembly only has been renewed as there may be slight manufacturing tolerance differences which could affect the steering alignment dimensions.

12 Steering idler - inspection and overhaul

1   If movement is detected between the idler arm shaft and the rubber bushes which are pressed into the idler shaft carrier, then the unit must be dismantled and new components fitted (photo).
2   Disconnect the trackrod-end and centre rod ball joints from the idler arm as described in the preceding Section.
3   Unbolt and remove the idler assembly from the bodyframe.
4   Unscrew the nut from the base of the idler shaft and withdraw the shaft. Inspect the surface of the shaft for scoring and if evident renew the shaft.
5   Press the bushes from the carrier and install new ones.
6   Reassemble the shaft, but do not fully tighten the nut at this stage.
7   Bolt the idler assembly to the bodyframe and reconnect the steering trackrod to the idler arm while the roadwheels are in the 'straight-ahead' position. This will mean that the idler arm will also be positioned so that it faces towards the front of the car parallel with the car centre-line.
8   Now tighten the idler shaft nut to a torque wrench setting of 50 lb f ft (69 Nm).
9   Where other new steering linkage components have been fitted, do not tighten the idler shaft nut until the front wheel alignment has been checked and adjusted and the front roadwheels set in the 'straight-ahead' position.

Fig. 10.19. Exploded view of one side of the rear suspension

1 Spring insulator
2 Seat
3 Spring
4 Control arm
5 Bracket
6 Pivot bolt
7 Plain washer
8 Plain washer
9 Lockwasher
10 Bolt
11 Plain washer
12 Flexible bush
13 Lockwasher
14 Nut
15 Nut
16 Lockwasher
17 Plain washer
18 Rebound stop
19 Nut
20 Lockwasher
21 Plain washer
22 Cushion
23 Shock absorber
24 Plain washer
25 Cushion
26 Plain washers
27 Lockwasher
28 Nut

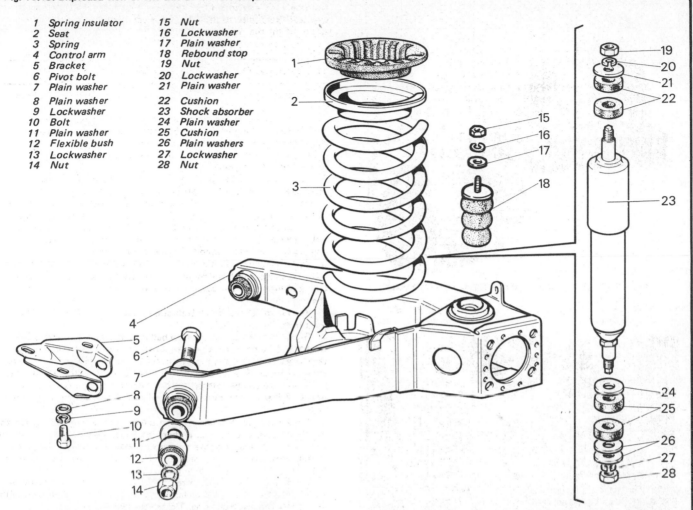

Fig. 10.20. Steering linkage (left-hand drive pinion)

1 Steering box
2 Idler arm assembly
3 Steering and idler drop arms
4 Centre track rod
5 Outer track rods

13 Steering wheel - removal and refitting

1 Disconnect the lead from the battery negative terminal.
2 Prise off the horn button from the centre of the steering wheel.
3 Relieve the staking on the now exposed nut and unscrew and remove it.
4 Turn the steering wheel if necessary to set the roadwheels in the 'straightahead' position and then pull the wheel from the steering shaft splines. If it is stuck tight, jar it off using the palms of the hands on the rear of the spokes.
5 Before refitting the steering wheel, apply a little grease to the shaft splines. Push the wheel into position and tighten a new nut using hand-pressure on the socket wrench only.
6 Reconnect the battery and drive the car along a straight section of road and check that the steering wheel spokes are horizontal or at least in an attitude to suit the driver.
7 Now tighten the nut to a torque wrench setting of 36 lb f ft (50 Nm) and stake the nut.
8 Refit the horn button.

14 Steering column - removal and installation

1 Set the roadwheels in the 'straight-ahead' position and disconnect the battery.
2 Working within the car, mark the position of the steering shaft upper and lower universal joint couplings in relation to the shaft. Use quick drying paint or scribe lines to do this (photo).
3 Remove the steering wheel, as described in the preceding Section.
4 Insert a screwdriver into the hole on the lower surface of the steering column shroud and release the screw which secures the direction indicator switch.
5 Disconnect the wiring harness multipin plugs and withdraw the column switches.
6 Extract the securing screws from the steering column shroud and withdraw it upwards.
7 Unscrew and remove the pinch bolt from the steering shaft upper coupling.
8 Unscrew and remove the nuts which secure the steering column upper bracket to the instrument panel (Fig. 10.21).
9 Withdraw the steering column.
10 The steering shaft lower coupling can be released if required by removing its pinch bolt and the lower shaft assembly detached from the steering box pinion shaft.
11 Installation is a reversal of removal, but do not tighten the upper bracket nuts until the universal coupling pinch bolts are fully engaged in their grooves in the splined sections of the shafts and the nuts tightened.

15 Steering column - overhaul

1 Wear in the steering shaft universal joint couplings can only be rectified by renewal of the complete shaft assembly (Fig. 10.22).
2 The rubber bushes in the upper bracket can be renewed, but when installing the new ones, make sure that the slots in them are not in alignment with the staking tags of the bracket.
3 If the steering column lock assembly must be removed because of a fault, or if the keys have been lost, then the shear type bolts must be drilled out or the bolts cut by carefully inserting a hacksaw blade between the joint of the lock half sections. When installing the new lock assembly do not fully tighten the securing bolts until the key has been turned to check that the lock tongue is in correct alignment with the notch in the steering upper shaft.
4 When the operation of the steering lock is satisfactory, fully tighten the shear bolts to break off their heads.

Fig. 10.21. Steering column securing nuts (1) and upper coupling pinch bolt (2)

12.1 Steering idler assembly

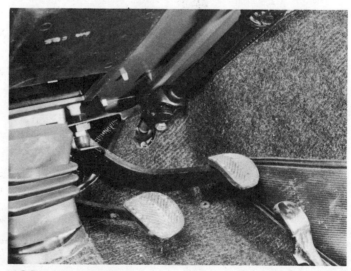

14.2 Steering column shaft

16 Steering box - removal, overhaul and installation

1 Set the roadwheels in the 'straight-ahead' position with the car over an inspection pit or the front of it raised on ramps or stands.

2 Working inside the car, mark the alignment of the steering shaft lower coupling to the splined pinion shaft of the steering box and then extract the coupling pinch bolt.

3 Working under the car, disconnect the centre and outer trackrod-end ball joints from the steering drop arm (photo).

4 Unscrew and remove the steering box mounting nuts and remove the box from the bodyframe. If it appears stuck, carefully prise the jaws of the steering shaft lower coupling apart with a large screwdriver.

5 Clean away external dirt, unscrew the combined oil filler/level plug and drain the oil.

6 Secure the steering box in the jaws of a vice.

7 Undo the bolt holding the drop arm to the drop arm shaft and pull it off. An extractor will be needed for this (Fig. 10.23).

8 Remove the screws holding the steering box cover and remove that (Fig. 10.29).

9 Take out the sector attached to the drop arm shaft. With it may come the eccentric bush. Between the sector and the casing is a thick thrust washer. Note the small peg that prevents the thrust washer from turning, sticking out from the body of the steering box. Also there are likely to be shims between the thrust washer and the steering box.

10 Remove the split pin from the castellated cap at the bottom of the worm shaft.

11 Unscrew the castellated cap. Long nosed pliers can be used for this if the special tool is not available. With the cap removed the worm should be tapped very gently on the end of the shaft where the steering column is attached. This will drive out the race for the bottom taper roller bearing. Once this is removed the worm with the two inner races can be removed. Note there is a seal inside the top race mounted in the steering box. This stops oil coming out upwards to the shaft. The seal for the bottom is the castellated cap.

12 Inspect all components and renew any that are worn.

13 Reassemble the steering box by reversing the dismantling operations but observe the following precautions and adjustment.

14 Before installing the worm, check that the upper oil seal is in good condition, otherwise renew it.

15 Before fitting the thrust washer for the sector, put in shims as needed to get the centre line of the sector's teeth level with the centre line of the worm. Then put in the thrust washer, locating its cut out with the peg in the box.

16 An oil seal goes round the drop arm shaft at the bottom of the eccentric bush inside the serrated adjustment plate. After the plate is a metal shield with a dirt seal.

17 Backlash between the worm and sector is controlled by an eccentric bush. The bush is moved by the adjuster plate which should be turned within the limits of its elongated bolt holes. This action moves the sector on top of the drop arm shaft closer to the worm. If the range of adjustment provided by the holes in the adjuster plate is insufficient, lift the plate and move it round a few splines (photo).

18 The ideal setting is for the sector to have all free-play eliminated when the steering drop arm is in the 'straight-ahead' position. The drop arm will of course have been removed but this position can be determined by reference to the master spline on the drop arm shaft.

19 The endfloat in the drop arm shaft is corrected by a peg screwed into the top of the steering box. This is held by a locknut. Slacken the locknut. Screw in the peg until it is in light contact with the sector underneath the cover. Hold it there and tighten the locknut. Note this adjustment must also be done with the steering in the 'straight-ahead' position. On the road, the need for this adjustment can be detected sometimes by a clonking heard or felt in the steering wheel on bad bumps taken slowly. It can be felt in bad cases when pulling or pushing the drop arm from beneath the car (photo).

20 The endfloat in the worm, which is the extension of the steering column in the box, is adjusted by the castellated cap in the bottom of the box (photo).

21 Take out the split pin. Screw up the cap, using long nosed pliers opened wide, till all endfloat goes. But do not overtighten. There should be no stiffness.

22 Insert the split pin into whichever of the two holes lines up best.

23 This endfloat should not need resetting in service, but will need adjustment after the box is stripped.

24 Install the steering box, engaging the lower coupling of the steering shaft in the previously marked alignment position while the steering drop arm shaft master spline is also in the 'straight-ahead' attitude.

25 Tighten the steering box mounting nuts and the coupling pinch bolt.

26 Refit the drop arm. This can only go on in one position as it has a master spline/groove arrangement.

27 Reconnect the trackrod-end ball joints to the steering drop arm.

28 Refill the steering box to the correct level with the specified oil.

Note: The adjustments described in this Section can be carried out if necessary at times when overhaul is not required and without removing the box from the car. It is important however, to disconnect the trackrod-end ball joints from the drop arm if worm to sector backlash is being checked in order to remove any external influence on the precise setting which must be achieved.

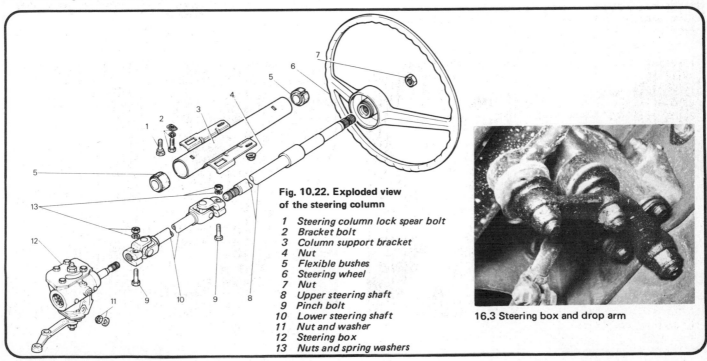

Fig. 10.22. Exploded view of the steering column

1   Steering column lock spear bolt
2   Bracket bolt
3   Column support bracket
4   Nut
5   Flexible bushes
6   Steering wheel
7   Nut
8   Upper steering shaft
9   Pinch bolt
10 Lower steering shaft
11 Nut and washer
12 Steering box
13 Nuts and spring washers

16.3 Steering box and drop arm

16.17 Steering worm and sector backlash adjuster plate

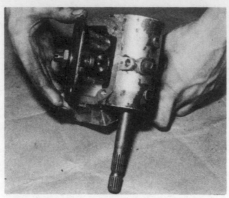

16.19 Steering box cover, adjuster and locknut

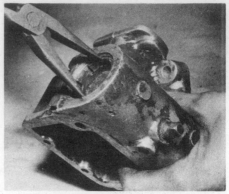

16.20 Turning the worm endfloat adjuster cap

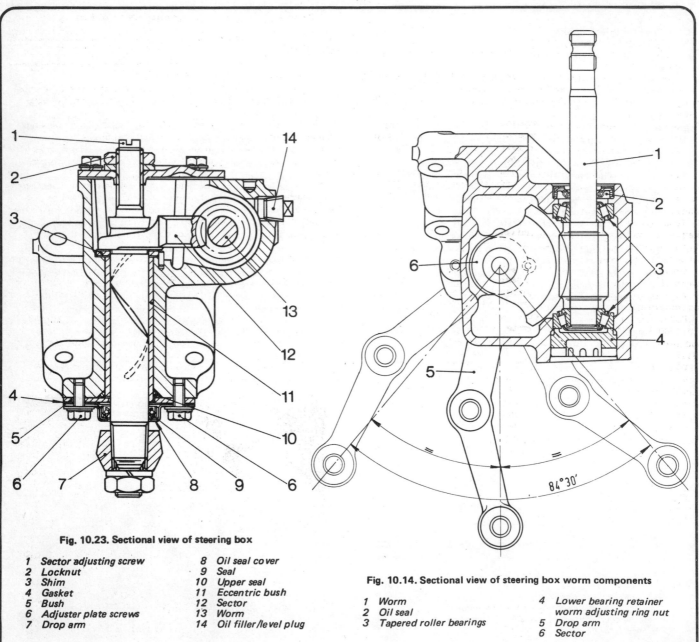

Fig. 10.23. Sectional view of steering box

1	Sector adjusting screw	8	Oil seal cover
2	Locknut	9	Seal
3	Shim	10	Upper seal
4	Gasket	11	Eccentric bush
5	Bush	12	Sector
6	Adjuster plate screws	13	Worm
7	Drop arm	14	Oil filler/level plug

Fig. 10.14. Sectional view of steering box worm components

1	Worm	4	Lower bearing retainer worm adjusting ring nut
2	Oil seal	5	Drop arm
3	Tapered roller bearings	6	Sector

17 Steering angles and front wheel alignment

1   Accurate front wheel alignment is essential for good steering and tyre wear. Before considering the steering angle, check that the tyres are correctly inflated, that the front wheels are not buckled, the hub bearings are not worn or incorrectly adjusted and that the steering linkage is in good order, without slackness or wear at the joints.

2   Wheel alignment consists of four factors:

Camber, which is the angle at which the front wheels are set from the vertical when viewed from the front of the car. Positive camber is the amount (in degrees) that the wheels are tilted outwards at the top from the vertical.

Castor is the angle between the steering axis and a vertical line when viewed from each side of the car. Positive castor is when the steering axis is inclined rearward.

Steering axis inclination is the angle, when viewed from the front of the car, between the vertical and an imaginary line drawn through the king pins.

Toe-in is the amount by which the distance between the front inside edges of the roadwheels (measured at hub height) is less than the diametrically opposite distance measured between the rear inside edges of the front roadwheels.

3   It is recommended that steering angles other than toe-in are checked and adjusted by your Fiat dealer as special gauges are required. However, it is worth knowing the method of adjusting the camber and castor angles.

4   To adjust the camber angle, release the suspension upper control arm pivot shaft from the bodyframe as fully described in Section 8 of this Chapter and add or remove an equal number of shims from each securing stud. Adding shims increases the camber angle.

5   To adjust the castor angle, again release the suspension upper control arm pivot shaft from the bodyframe and transfer shims from one securing stud to the other. To increase the castor angle, transfer shims from the rear to the front stud.

6   To adjust the front wheel toe-in, place the car on level ground, with the tyres correctly inflated and loaded with the weight of four people. An alternative to this is to load the car with the equivalent weight of concrete blocks placed on the floor of the car and evenly distributed.

7   Obtain or make a toe-in (tracking) gauge. One can be made from a length of tubing having an adjustable setscrew and nut at one end.

8   With the gauge, measure the distance between the two inner rims of the front roadwheels, at hub height and at the rear of the wheels.

9   Pull or push the vehicle so that the roadwheel turns through half a turn (180°) and measure the distance between the two inner rims at hub height at the front of the wheel. This last measurement should be less than the first by the specified toe-in (see Specifications Section).

10   When the toe-in is found to be incorrect, slacken the clamp nuts on each outer trackrod and rotate each trackrod an equal amount but in opposite directions, until the correct toe-in is obtained. Tighten the clamp nuts ensuring that the ball joints are held in the centre of their arc of travel during tightening. If new trackrods or ball joints have been fitted, a starting point for adjusting the front wheel alignment is to set each outer trackrod so that the distance measured between the centres of the ball joint taper pins is equal with the roadwheels in the 'straight-ahead' position.

18 Steering lock angles

1   These angles are not adjustable, but should conform to the angles given in the Specifications Section.

2   In the event of the front tyres scraping on the suspension or bodywork during full lock, this will be due to one of three causes and should be rectified immediately.

a)   *Collision damage to components.*
b)   *Severe wear in suspension or steering components*
c)   *Grossly inaccurate steering angles or front wheel alignment (toe-in).*

19 Rear wheel alignment

1   The rear roadwheels toe-in by the amount given in the Specifications Section.

2   Care should always be taken to mark the exact position of the rear suspension control arms before unbolting them from the bodyframe (see Section 9, paragraph 8) so that they can be refitted without upsetting the toe-in.

3   Special equipment is needed to check the rear wheel toe-in and this is best left to your dealer. In an emergency, an approximate setting can be obtained if the front wheels are set exactly in the 'straight-ahead' position and a straight edge is then placed in contact with the front and rear tyre walls on one side of the car. Load the car with (or the equivalent of) four people.

4   Adjust the rear wheel toe-in so that the wall of the tyre at the front of the rear roadwheel shows a gap between it and the straight edge of **half** of the specified toe-in. Adjustment is carried out by releasing the control arm to bodyframe bolts and moving the control arm within the limits of the elongated bolt holes. If the range of adjustment is insufficient, then the adjustment shims which are located on either side of the control arm pivot bolt will have to be transferred from one side to the other as required (Fig. 10.25).

5   Repeat the operations on the opposite rear roadwheel.

20 Wheels and tyres

1   The roadwheels are of pressed steel type.

2   Periodically remove the wheels, clean dirt and mud from the inside and outside surfaces and examine for signs of rusting or rim damage and rectify as necessary.

3   Apply a smear of light grease to the wheel bolts before screwing them in and finally tighten them to the specified torque.

4   The tyres fitted are of radial ply construction. Never mix tyres of different construction and always check and maintain the pressures regularly.

5   If the wheels have been balanced on the vehicle then it is important that the wheels are not moved round the vehicle in an effort to equalise tread wear. If a wheel is removed, then the relationship of the hub to the holes in the wheel should be marked to ensure exact replacement otherwise the balance of wheel, hub and tyre will be upset.

6   Where the wheels have been balanced off the vehicle, then they may be moved round to equalise wear. Include the spare wheel in any rotational pattern. With radial ply tyres, do not move the wheels from side to side but only interchange the front and rear wheels on the same side.

7   Balancing of the wheels is an essential factor in good steering and road holding. When the tyres have been in use for about half their useful life the wheels should be rebalanced to compensate for the lost tread rubber due to wear.

8   Inspect the tyre walls and treads regularly for cuts and damage and where evident, have them professionally repaired.

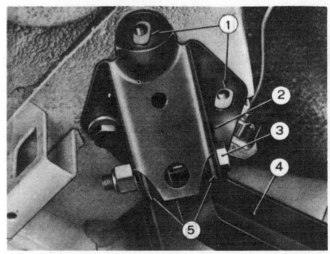

Fig. 10.25. Rear suspension control arm bracket showing elongated bolt holes for toe-in adjustment

1 Holes	4 Control arm
2 Bracket	5 Adjustment shims
3 Pivot bolt	

21 Fault diagnosis - suspension and steering

Symptom	Reason/s
Steering feels vague, car wanders and floats at speed	Tyre pressure uneven. Shock absorbers worn. Spring broken. Steering gear balljoints badly worn. Suspension geometry incorrect. Steering mechanism free play excessive. Front suspension and rear control arm pick-up points out of alignment.
Stiff and heavy steering	Tyre pressures too low. No grease in king pin bushes. Seized steering and suspension balljoints. Front wheel toe-in incorrect. Suspension geometry incorrect. Steering gear incorrectly adjusted too tightly.
Wheel wobble and vibration	Wheel bolts loose. Front wheels and tyres out of balance. Steering balljoints badly worn. Hub bearings badly worn. Steering gear free play excessive. Front spring weak or broken.

Chapter 11 Body and fittings

Contents

1 General description

1 The Fiat 126 is produced in one body style - a two door four seater saloon.

2 Construction is of welded, all steel integral body and underframe or floorpan.

3 General trim and equipment is adequate without luxury features and the keynote of controls and accessories is one of simplicity.

4 Apart from the engine compartment and luggage boot lids and the doors, no other body panels are detachable and in the event of damage of a serious nature, the panel will have to be cut away and a new one welded into place.

2 Maintenance - bodywork and underframe

1 The general condition of a car's bodywork is the one thing that significantly affects its value. Maintenance is easy but needs to be regular and particular. Neglect, particularly after minor damage, can lead quickly to further deterioration and costly repair bills. It is important also to keep watch on those parts of the car not immediately visible, for instance, the underside, inside all the wheel arches and the lower part of the engine compartment.

2 The basic maintenance routine for the bodywork is washing - preferably with a lot of water, from a hose. This will remove all the loose solids which may have stuck to the car. It is important to flush these off in such a way as to prevent grit from scratching the finish. The wheel arches and underbody need washing in the same way to remove any accumulated mud which will retain moisture and tend to encourage rust. Parodoxically enough, the best time to clean the underbody and wheel arches is in wet weather when the mud is thoroughly wet and soft. In very wet weather the underbody is usually cleaned of large accumulations automatically and this is a good time for inspection.

3 Periodically it is a good idea to have the whole of the underside of the car steam cleaned, engine compartment included, so that a thorough inspection can be carried out to see what minor repairs and renovations are necessary. Steam cleaning is available at many garages and is necessary for removal of accumulation of oily grime which sometimes is allowed to cake thick in certain areas near the engine, gearbox and back axle. If steam facilities are not available, there are one or two excellent grease solvents available which can be brush applied. The dirt can then be simply hosed off.

4 After washing paintwork, wipe off with a chamois leather to give an unspotted clear finish. A coat of clear protective wax polish will give added protection against chemical pollutants in the air. If the paintwork sheen has dulled or oxidised, use a cleaner/polish combination to restore the brilliance of the shine. This requires a little more effort, but is usually caused because regular washing has been neglected. Always check that door and ventilator opening drain holes and pipes are completely clear so that water can drain out. Bright work should be treated the same way as paintwork. Windscreens and windows can be kept clear of the smeary film which often appears, if a little ammonia is added to the water. If they are scratched, a good rub with a proprietary metal polish will often clear them. Never use any form of wax or other body or chromium polish on glass.

3 Maintenance - upholstery and carpets

1 Mats and carpets should be brushed or vacuum cleaned regularly to keep them free of grit. If they are badly stained remove them from the car for scrubbing or sponging and make quite sure they are dry before replacement. Seats and interior trim panels can be kept clean by a wipe over with a damp cloth. If they do become stained (which can be more apparent on light coloured upholstery) use a little detergent and a soft nail brush to scour the grime out of the grain of the material. Do not forget to keep the head lining clean in the same way as the upholstery. When using liquid cleaners inside the car do not over-wet the surface being cleaned. Excessive damp could get into the seams and padded interior causing stains, offensive odours or even rot. If the inside of the car gets wet accidentally it is worthwhile taking some trouble to dry it out properly, particularly where carpets are involved. **Do not** leave oil or electric heaters inside the car for this purpose.

4   Minor body damage - repair

See also photo sequences on pages 110 and 111.

Repair of minor scratches in the car's bodywork

If the scratch is very superficial, and does not penetrate to the metal of the bodywork repair is very simple. Lightly rub the area of the scratch with a paintwork renovator, or a very fine cutting paste, to remove loose paint from the scratch and to clear the surrounding bodywork of wax polish. Rinse the area with clean water.

Apply touch-up paint to the scratch using a thin paint brush; continue to apply thin layers of paint until the surface of the paint in the scratch is level with surrounding paintwork. Allow the new paint at least two weeks to harden; then, blend it into the surrounding paintwork by rubbing the paintwork in the scratch area with a paintwork renovator or a very fine cutting paste. Finally apply wax polish.

Where a scratch has penetrated, right through to the metal of the bodywork, causing the metal to rust, a different repair technique is required. Remove any loose rust from the bottom of the scratch with a penknife, then apply rust inhibiting paint to prevent the formation of rust in the future. Using a rubber or nylon applicator fill the scratch with bodystopper paste. If required, this paste can be mixed with cellulose thinners to provide a very thin paste which is ideal for filling narrow scratches. Before the stopper-paste in the scratch hardens, wrap a piece of smooth cotton rag around the tip of the finger; dip the finger in cellulose thinners and then quickly sweep it across the surface of the stopper-paste in the scratch; this will ensure that the surface of the stopper-paste is slightly hollowed. Tne scratch can now be painted over as described earlier in this Section.

Repair of dents in the car's bodywork

When deep denting of the car's bodywork has taken place, the first task is to pull the dent out, until the affected bodywork almost attains its original shape. There is little point in trying to restore the original shape completely, as the metal in the damaged area will have stretched on impact and cannot be reshaped fully to its original contour. It is better to bring the level of the dent up to a point which is about 1/8 in (3 mm) below the level of the surrounding bodywork. In cases where the dent is very shallow anyway, it is not worth trying to pull it out at all.

If the underside of the dent is accessible, it can be hammered out gently from behind, using a mallet with a wooden or plastic head. Whilst doing this, hold a suitable block of wood firmly against the outside of the dent. This block will absorb the impact from the hammer blows and thus prevent a large area of bodywork from being 'belled-out.'

Should the dent be in a section of the bodywork which has a double skin or some other factor making it inaccessible from behind, a different technique is called for. Drill several small holes through the metal inside the dent area - particularly in the deeper sections. Then screw long self-tapping screws into the holes just sufficiently for them to gain a good purchase in the metal. Now the dent can be pulled out by pulling on the protruding heads of the screws with a pair of pliers.

The next stage of the repair is the removal of the paint from the damaged area, and from an inch or so of the surrounding 'sound' bodywork. This is accomplished most easily by using a wire brush or abrasive pad on a power drill, although it can be done just as effectively by hand using sheets of abrasive paper. To complete the preparations for filling, score the surface of the bare metal with a screwdriver or the tang of a file, or alternatively, drill small holes in the affected area. This will provide a really good 'key' for the filler paste.

To complete the repair see the Section on filling and respraying.

Repair of rust holes or gashes in the car's bodywork

Remove all paint from the affected area and from an inch or so of the surrounding 'sound' bodywork, using an abrasive pad or a wire brush on a power drill. If these are not available a few sheets of abrasive paper will do the job just as effectively. With the paint removed you will be able to gauge the severity of the corrosion and therefore decide whether to replace the whole panel (if this is possible) or to repair the affected area. Replacement body panels are not as expensive as most people think and it is often quicker and more satisfactory to fit a new panel than to attempt to repair areas of corrosion.

Remove all fittings from the affected area, except those which will act as a guide to the original shape of the damaged bodywork (eg. headlamp shells etc). Then, using tin snips or a hacksaw blade, remove all loose metal and any other metal badly affected by corrosion. Hammer the edges of the hole inwards in order to create a slight depression for the filler paste.

Wire brush the affected area to remove the powdery rust from the surface of the remaining metal. Paint the affected area with rust inhibiting paint, if the back of the rusted area is accessible treat this also.

Before filling can take place it will be necessary to block the hole in some way. This can be achieved by the use of one of the following materials: Zinc gauze, Aluminium tape or Polyurethan foam.

Zinc gauze is probably the best material to use for a large hole. Cut a piece to the approximate size and shape of the hole to be filled, then position it in the hole so that its edges are below the level of the surrounding bodywork. It can be retained in position by several blobs of filler paste around its periphery.

Aluminium tape should be used for small or very narrow holes. Pull a piece off the roll and trim it to the approximate size and shape required, then pull off the backing paper (if used) and stick the tape over the hole; it can be overlapped if the thickness of one piece is insufficient. Burnish down the edges of the tape with the handle of a screwdriver or similar, to ensure that the tape is securely attached to the metal underneath.

Polyurethane foam is best used where the holes are situated in a section of bodywork of complex shape, backed by a small box section (eg. where the sill panel meets the rear wheel arch - most cars). The usual mixing procedure for this foam is as follows: Put equal amounts of fluid from each of the two cans provided in the kit, into one container. Stir until the mixture begins to thicken, then quickly pour this mixture into the hole, and hold a piece of cardboard over the larger apertures. Almost immediately the polyurethane will begin to expand, gushing out of any small holes left unblocked. When the foam hardens it can be cut back to just below the level of the surrounding bodywork with a hacksaw blade.

Bodywork repairs - filling and re-spraying

Before using this Section, see the Sections on dent, deep scratch, rust hole, and gash repairs.

Many types of bodyfiller are available, but generally speaking those proprietary kits which contain a tin of filler paste and a tube of resin hardener are best for this type of repair. A wide, flexible plastic or nylon applicator will be found invaluable for imparting a smooth and well contoured finish to the surface of the filler.

Mix up a little filler on a clean piece of card or board - use the hardener sparingly (follow the maker's instructions on the packet), otherwise the filler will set very rapidly.

Using the applicator, apply the filler paste to the prepared area; draw the applicator across the surface of the filler to achieve the correct contour and to level the filler surface. As soon as a contour that approximates the correct one is achieved stop working the paste. If you carry on too long the paste will become sticky and begin to 'pick-up' on the applicator. Continue to add thin layers of filler paste at twenty-minute intervals until the level of the filler is just 'proud' of the the surrounding bodywork.

Once the filler has hardened, excess can be removed using a metal plane or coarse file. From then on, progressively finer grades of abrasive paper should be used, starting with a 40 grade production paper and finishing with 400 grade wet or dry paper. Always wrap the abrasive paper around a flat rubber, cork, or wooden block - otherwise the surface of the filler will not be completely flat. During the smoothing of the filler surface the wet or dry paper should be periodically rinsed in water; this will ensure that a very smooth finish is imparted to the filler at the final stage.

At this stage the 'dent' should be surrounded by a ring of bare metal, which in turn should be encircled by a finely 'feathered' edge of the good paintwork. Rinse the repair area with clean water, until all of the dust produced by the rubbing-down operation is gone.

Spray the whole repair area with a light coat of grey primer - this will show up any imperfections in the surface of the filler. Repair these imperfections with fresh filler paste or bodystopper, and once more smooth the surface with abrasive paper. If bodystopper is used, it can be mixed with cellulose thinners to form a really thin paste which is ideal for filling small holes. Repeat this spray and repair procedure until you are satisfied that the surface of the filler, and the feathered edge of the paintwork are perfect. Clean the repair area with clean water and allow to dry fully.

The repair area is now ready for spraying. Paint spraying must be carried out in a warm, dry, windless and dust free atmosphere. This condition can be created artificially if you have access to a large indoor working area, but if you are forced to work in the open, you will have to pick your day very carefully. If you are working indoors, dousing the floor in the work area with water will 'lay' the dust which would otherwise be in the atmosphere. If the repair area is confined to one body panel, mask off the surrounding panels; this will help to minimise the effect of a slight mis-match in paint colours. Bodywork fittings (eg. chrome strips, door handles etc) will also need to be masked off. Use genuine masking tape and several thicknesses of newspaper for the masking operation.

Before commencing to spray, agitate the aerosol can thoroughly, then spray a test area (an old tin, or similar) until the technique is mastered. Cover the repair area with a thick coat of primer; the thickness should be built up using several thin layers of paint rather than one thick one. Using 400 grade wet or dry paper, rub down the surface of the primer until it is really smooth. While doing this, the work area should be thoroughly doused with water, and the wet or dry paper periodically rinsed in water. Allow to dry before spraying on more paint.

Spray on the top coat, again building up the thickness by using several thin layers of paint. Start spraying in the centre of the repair area and then, using a circular motion, work outwards until the whole repair area and about 2 inches of the surrounding original paintwork is covered. Remove all masking material 10 to 15 minutes after spraying on the final coat of paint.

Allow the new paint at least 2 weeks to harden fully; then, using a paintwork renovator or a very fine cutting paste, blend the edges of the new paint into the existing paintwork. Finally, apply wax polish.

5 Major body damage - repair

Where serious damage has occurred or large areas need renewal due to neglect, it means certainly that completely new sections or panels will need welding in and this is best left to professionals. If the damage is due to impact it will also be necessary to completely check the alignment of the bodyshell structure. Due to the principle of construction the strength and shape of the whole can be affected by damage to a part. In such instances the services of a Fiat dealer with specialist checking jigs are essential. If a body is left misaligned it is first of all dangerous as the car will not handle properly and secondly uneven stresses will be imposed on the steering, engine and transmission causing abnormal wear or complete failure. Tyre wear may also be excessive.

6 Maintenance - hinges and locks

1   Oil the hinges of the engine compartment lid, boot and doors with a drop or two of light oil periodically. A good time is after the car has been washed.
2   Oil the luggage boot release catch pivot pin and the safety catch pivot pin periodically.
3   Do not over lubricate door latches and strikers. Normally a little oil on the rotary cam spindle alone is sufficient.

7 Door interior trim panel - removal and refitting

1   Open the door wide and prise off the escutcheon plate from the door interior handle (photo).
2   Insert a piece of wire with a hook at the end behind the window regulator handle and pull out the handle securing clip. Remove the regulator handle (photo).
3   Unscrew and remove the two upper securing screws from the map pocket (photo).
4   Insert the fingers between the trim panel and the door at its upper edge and pull the panel away to disengage the securing clips. Work the fingers all round the edge of the panel until it can be removed from the door. Pull away the waterproof sheet (photo).
5   Refitting is a reversal of removal, but when installing the window

regulator handle, note how to locate the spring clip and then simply tap the handle onto the splines of the spindle by giving it a bang with the palm of the hand. The clip will engage in the groove in the spindle and lock the handle in position (photo).

8 Door lock - removal, refitting and adjustment

1   Open the door wide and remove the interior trim panel as described in the preceding Section.
2   Unscrew and remove the knob from the lock plunger (Fig. 11.1).
3   Unscrew and remove the screws which secure the door interior remote control handle and its baseplate.
4   Disconnect the link rod vibration insulator.
5   Disconnect the link rod from the door exterior handle.
6   Unscrew and remove the securing bolts which retain the lock assembly. These are accessible on the door edge.
7   The complete lock assembly can now be withdrawn from the door cavity, manoeuvring the link rods through the door apertures or bringing them to a position where their connecting clips can be detached.
8   If the exterior handle must be removed, the securing nuts can be reached through the access hole in the inner panel (photo).
9   Refitting is a reversal of removal, but any adjustment required to ensure smooth positive closure is carried out by moving the position of the striker on the door pillar after having released the securing and adjustment screws (Fig. 11.2).

9 Window regulator mechanism - removal and refitting

1   Remove the door interior trim panel, as previously described.
2   Before dismantling the cable assembly, cut two thin blocks of wood and insert them between the cable drum and its support bracket to prevent the cable unwinding from the drum (Fig. 11.3).
3   Disconnect the cable clamp at the glass lift channel. It is a good idea to mark the position of the cable at the clamp to assist when refitting (photo).
4   Push the glass well up and support it.
5   Unbolt the regulator unit from the door and then release the cable from the pulleys. Withdraw the mechanism from the door cavity (Fig. 11.4).
6   If the cable is not to be renewed, the assembly can be refitted by reversing the removal operations. Refit the cable clamp in its original position and any retensioning which may be necessary can be carried out by releasing the securing screw and moving the position of the tensioner pulley.
7   If a new cable is to be fitted, wind the new cable round the drum so that the part of the cable which leaves the drum in a downward direction is located in the groove of the drum nearest the door inner panel.
8   Engage the cable round the pulleys, bolt the regulator unit into position, tension the cable and then connect the cable clamp with the glass in its fully lowered position. Check the operation of the window by temporarily refitting the regulator handle and readjust the position of the cable clamp if necessary.

10 Door glass - removal and refitting

1   Remove the window regulator mechanism as described in paragraphs 1 to 5 of the preceding Section.
2   Push the window glass fully up and unbolt and remove the glass front channel (Fig. 11.5).
3   Lower the glass carefully and withdraw it downwards and outwards from the door cavity.
4   If a new door glass is being installed, make sure that the lift channel is located directly in the centre of the glass and the rubber insulator between channel and glass is firmly stuck in position.
5   Install the glass and regulator by reversing the removal operations.

7.1 Removing door remote control handle escutcheon

7.2 Removing window regulator handle

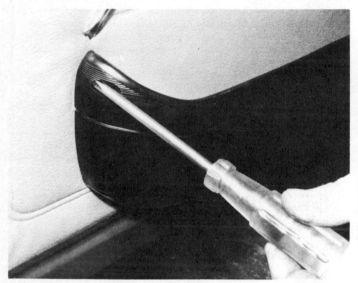

7.3 Removing a map pocket screw

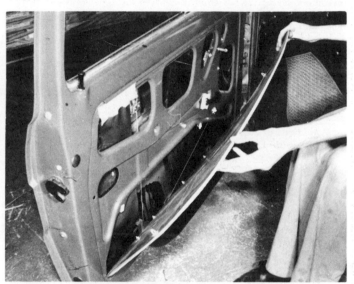

7.4 Removing the door interior trim panel

7.5 Window regulator handle securing clip

8.8 View of door exterior handle from within door cavity

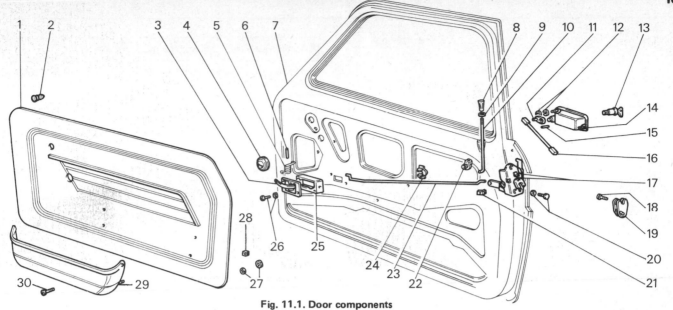

Fig. 11.1. Door components

1	Trim panel	7	Door	13	Lock cylinder
2	Panel clip	8	Plunger knob	14	Exterior door handle
3	Lock remote control handle	9	Grommet	15	Pin
4	Escutcheon plate	10	Lock control rod	16	Connecting rod
5	Return springs	11	Link plate	17	Lock assembly
6	Pivot pin	12	Washers	18	Screw
				19	Striker
				20	Screw and washer
				21	Connecting clips
				22	Connecting clips

23	Remote control rod
24	Control rod guide
25	Handle baseplate
26	Screw
27	Map pocket lower nut and washer
28	Captive nut
29	Map pocket
30	Map pocket upper screw

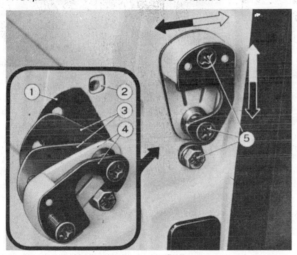

Fig. 11.2. Door striker assembly

1	Gasket	4	Striker
2	Captive tapped plate	5	Securing screws and bolt
3	Spacers		

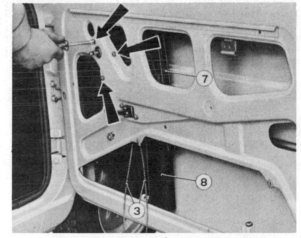

Fig. 11.4. Window regulator securing bolts (7) cable (3) and waterproof deflector (8)

Fig. 11.3. Window winding mechanism. Temporary cable retaining blocks (arrowed)

9.3 Window operating cable clamp

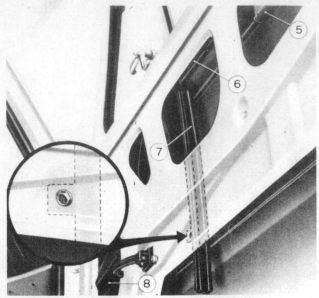

Fig. 11.5. Door glass front guide channel

5   Glass lift channel   7   Front guide channel
6   Glass   8   Waterproof deflector

11 Swivel ventilators - removal and refitting

1   Remove the main door glass, as described in the preceding Section.
2   Extract the two ventilator frame screws from the upper front door edge (Fig. 11.6).
3   Remove the main door glass rear guide channel which is secured to the inside of the door by two screws accessible on the door edge. This will enable the main glass rubber channel to be slid back by about 2 inches (50.8 mm) from its abutment with the ventilator vertical frame (Fig. 11.7).
4   Push in a wooden wedge to expand the weatherstrip and then move the ventilator assembly rearwards by tilting it at the top. Withdraw the ventilator from the door.
5   The ventilator upper hinge is rivetted and if the glass is to be renewed then it will have to be drilled out.
6   Refitting is a reversal of removal.

12 Window mouldings - removal and refitting

1   The window exterior mouldings can be removed after first prising off the clip from the butt joint (Fig. 11.9).
2   Pull the moulding from its retaining clips working carefully round the window frame.
3   If the interior mouldings are to be removed, note that their securing clips also retain the plastic sheeting which is used as a protective barrier inside the door cavity (Fig. 11.10).

13 Door - removal and installation

1   Open the door and using a pair of pliers, compress the two legs of the check link towards each other so that they can be released from the body pillar (photo).
2   Support the bottom edge of the door on blocks or a jack suitably insulated with pads of rag to prevent damage to the paintwork.
3   Mark the location of the hinge plates on the door pillar and then unbolt the hinges and remove the door (Fig. 11.11).
4   Installation is a reversal of removal. Any adjustment needed to set the door square within its frame or flush with the outer body panels can be carried out by moving the position of the hinges on the body pillar.
5   Check the door for smooth positive closure and if necessary, move the lock striker to achieve this, as described in Section 8.

14 Windscreen glass - removal and installation

1   This is one of the few jobs best left to the professionals. However, where it is decided to do the work yourself, carry out the following operations.
2   If the glass has been broken, carefully knock out all the crystals which remain attached to the rubber surround. Protect the surface of the paintwork of the luggage boot lid and cover the vents on the fascia panel. Retrieve your tax disc.
3   If the glass is intact but is to be removed for renewal of the rubber weathersealing surround then first disconnect the wiper arms.
4   Using a small screwdriver, prise out the bright moulding from the rubber windscreen surround.
5   Remove the interior mirror and then prise the rubber surround lip (at the inside top centre) from the body frame edge. Work in both directions and exert even pressure along the top part of the screen until it moves outwards. Have an assistant help with this work.
6   Thoroughly clean the windscreen recess of the bodyframe and examine the rubber surround. If it is cut or has perished or hardened or old pieces of sealant cannot easily be removed, then renew it.
7   Commence installation of the windscreen by locating the rubber surround to the glass. Fit a thin cord to the body seating groove of the rubber surround so that the two ends overlap at the top centre (Fig. 11.12).
8   Locate the windscreen accurately at the lower edge of its aperture with the two ends of the pull cord hanging inside the vehicle.
9   Have an assistant press on the glass from the outside and pull the two ends of the fitting cord evenly so that the combination of pressure and cord withdrawal will engage the rubber surround lip with the body flange (Fig. 11.13).
10 With the windscreen installed, inject black sealant into the space between the rubber and the glass and between the rubber and the body.
11 Refit the bright trim preferably using a tool similar to the one shown which has the effect of opening the lips of the rubber channel just before the rear part of the tool presses the trim into it (Fig. 11.14).
12 Clean off any excess sealant with a rag soaked in paraffin or white spirit.
13 Locate the lead to the interior lamp using a screwdriver to engage it behind the lip of the rubber surround (Fig. 11.15).

Fig. 11.6. Swivel ventilator upper fixing screws

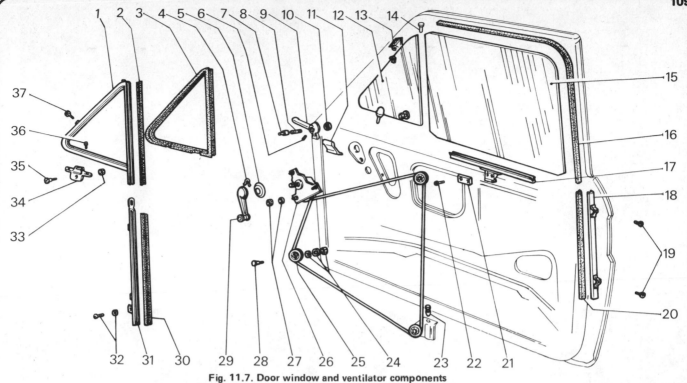

Fig. 11.7. Door window and ventilator components

1	Ventilator frame	10	Lockwasher
2	Rubber channel	11	Stop plate
3	Weather strip surround	12	Glass
4	Window regulator	13	Upper pivot
	handle spring clip	14	Rivet
5	Escutcheon plate	15	Window glass
6	Dowel	16	Rubber channel
7	Lock button	17	Glass lift channel
8	Spring	18	Rear guide channel
9	Lock lever	19	Screws

20	Rubber channel	29	Regulator handle
21	Cable clamp plate	30	Rubber channel
22	Screw	31	Front glass guide channel
23	Glass lower stop	32	Screw and washer
24	Nut and washers	33	Nut
25	Tensioner pulley	34	Ventilator lower pivot
26	Regulator assembly	35	Screw and washer
27	Nut and washer	36	Rivet
28	Pivot pin	37	Frame securing screw

Fig. 11.8. Removing a swivel ventilator

1	Rubber channel	3	Temporary wooden wedge
2	Frame		A = 2.0 in (50.8 mm)

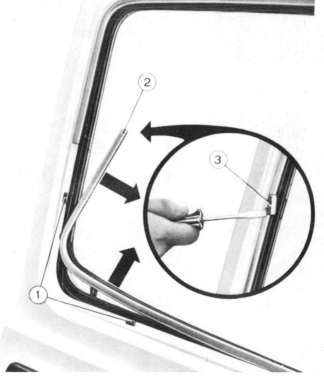

Fig. 11.9. Removing door window moulding

1	Retaining clips	3	Butt joint cover
2	Moulding		

This sequence of photographs deals with the repair of the dent and scratch (above rear lamp) shown in this photo. The procedure will be similar for the repair of a hole. It should be noted that the procedures given here are simplified - more explicit instructions will be found in the text

In the case of a dent the first job - after removing surrounding trim - is to hammer out the dent where access is possible. This will minimise filling. Here, the large dent having been hammered out, the damaged area is being made slightly concave

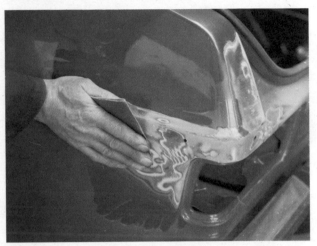

Now all paint must be removed from the damaged area, by rubbing with coarse abrasive paper. Alternatively, a wire brush or abrasive pad can be used in a power drill. Where the repair area meets good paintwork, the edge pf the paintwork should be 'feathered', using a finer grade of abrasive paper

In the case of a hole caused by rusting, all damaged sheet-metal should be cut away before proceeding to this stage. Here, the damaged area is being treated with rust remover and inhibitor before being filled

Mix the body filler according to its manufacturer's instructions. In the case of corrosion damage, it will be necessary to block off any large holes before filling - this can be done with zinc gauze or aluminium tape. Make sure the area is absolutely clean before ...

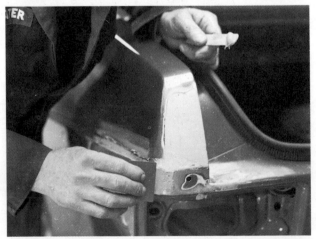

... applying the filler. Filler should be applied with a flexible applicator, as shown, for best results: the wooden spatula being used for confined areas. Apply thin layers of filler at 20-minute intervals, until the surface of the filler is slightly proud of the surrounding bodywork

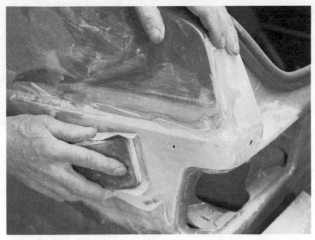

Initial shaping can be done with a Surform plane or Dreadnought file. Then, using progressively finer grades of wet-and-dry paper, wrapped around a sanding block, and copious amounts of clean water, rub-down the filler until really smooth and flat. Again, feather the edges of adjoining paintwork

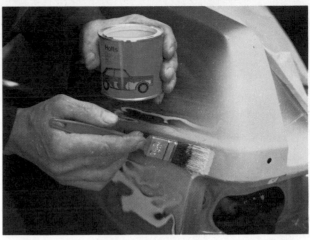

The whole repair area can now be sprayed or brush-painted with primer. If spraying, ensure adjoining areas are protected from over-spray. Note that at least one-inch of the surrounding sound paintwork should be coated with primer. Primer has a 'thick' consistency, so will fill small imperfections

Again, using plenty of water, rub down the primer with a fine grade of wet-and-dry paper (400 grade is probably best) until it is really smooth and well blended into the surrounding paint-work. Any remaining imperfections can now be filled by carefully applied knifing stopper paste

When the stopper has hardened, rub-down the repair area again before applying the final coat of primer. Before rubbing-down this last coat of primer, ensure the repair area is blemish-free - use more stopper if necessary. To ensure that the surface of the primer is really smooth use some finishing compound

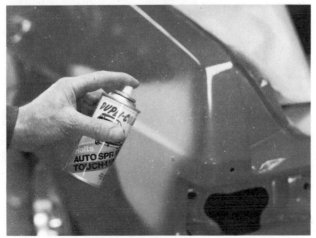

The top coat can now be applied. When working out of doors, pick a dry, warm and wind-free day. Ensure surrounding areas are protected from over-spray. Agitate the aerosol thoroughly, then spray the centre of the repair area, working outwards with a circular motion. Apply the paint as several thin coats.

After a period of about two-weeks, which the paint needs to harden fully, the surface of the repaired area can be 'cut' with a mild cutting compound prior to wax polishing. When carrying out bodywork repairs, remember that the quality of the finished job is proportional to the time and effort expended

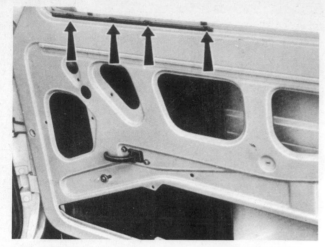

Fig. 11.10. Door waterproof deflector and moulding retainers

13.1 A door check strap

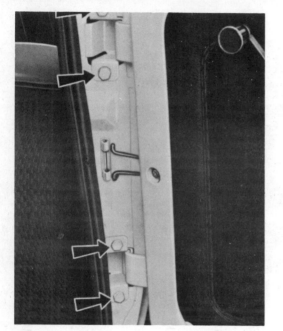

Fig. 11.11. Door hinge bolts on body pillar

Fig. 11.13. Installing windscreen

1 Glass   3 Body
2 Rubber surround

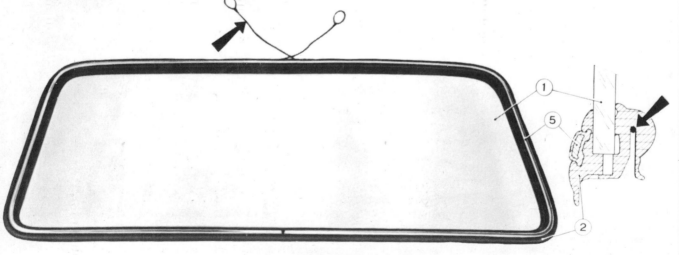

Fig. 11.12. Windscreen ready for installation

1 Glass   5 Fitting cord (arrowed)
2 Rubber surround

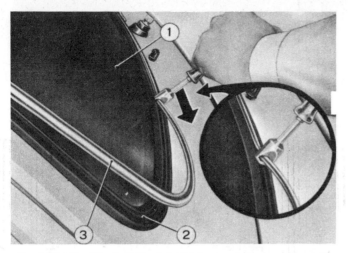

Fig. 11.14. Tool for installing bright trim to windscreen surround

1 Glass   3 Trim
2 Surround

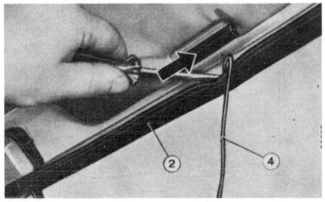

Fig. 11.15. Inserting lead to interior lamp under lip of windscreen rubber surround

2 Rubber surround   4 Lead

15 Rear window glass - removal and installation

1   The operations are very similar to those for the windscreen but exert pressure at the bottom of the glass to remove it outwards.
2   Install the glass using the cord method described in the preceding Section, but locate the glass to the upper edge of the aperture first and then press it evenly into position.

16 Fixed side windows - removal and installation

1   Remove and install just as described for the windscreen in Section 14, but push the glass out from one of the lower corners (Fig. 11.16).
2   Refit it by engaging the top of the rubber surround first.
3   Note the fitting of the drain tube bushes which are used to drain water which may have accumulated in the groove of the rubber surround (Fig. 11.17).

17 Opening side windows - removal and installation

1   Working inside the car, extract the two screws which secure the lock toggle to the body (Fig. 11.18).
2   Open the window to the maximum extent and disengage the hinges from the rubber grommets in the door pillar and lift the glass away (Fig. 11.19).
3   The glass can be pulled from the hinge clips.
4   Install by reversing the removal operations.

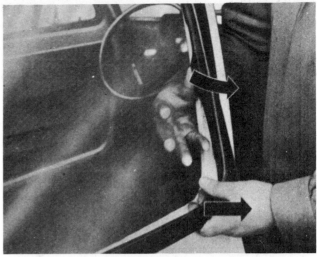

Fig. 11.16. Removing a side window

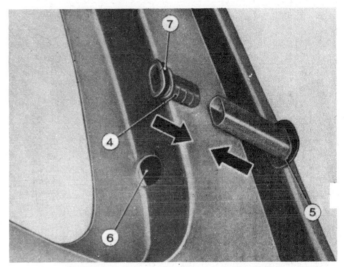

Fig. 11.17. Side window drain tube bushes

4 Bush component   6 Bush aperture
5 Bush component   7 Seal

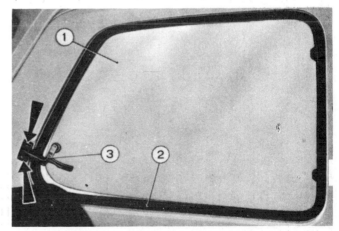

Fig. 11.18. Hinged type side window

1 Glass   3 Lock
2 Weather seal

Fig. 11.19. Removing opening type window glass

1   Glass   *2   Weather seal*

18 Luggage boot lid - removal and refitting

1   Open the lid to its fullest extent and have an assistant support it in this position (Fig. 11.20).
2   Loosen, but do not remove, the hinge securing screws and slide the lid towards the rear of the car and remove it. This is possible as the hinge bolts pass through open-ended slots not holes in the hinge plates.
3   Refit the lid by reversing the removal operations.
4   Any adjustment needed to ensure positive closure can be carried

out by moving the lid within the limits of the hinge plate slots.
5   When the lid alignment is correct, loosen the latch screws and move its position so that the striker pin on the boot lid engages centrally with the latch during closure.

19 Engine compartment lid - removal and refitting

1   Unscrew and remove the single self-locking nut from the right-hand hinge pin at the base of the lid (Fig. 11.21).
2   Open the lid and either prise up the tab of the check strap anchor to release the strap or unscrew and remove the single screw which anchors the other end of the check strap (photo).
3   Slide the lid sideways from its hinge pins.
4   Refit the lid by reversing the removal operations but any adjustment required to provide smooth positive closure should be carried out by releasing the bolts on the latch on the underside of the lid and moving the latch as necessary.

20 Fascia panel crash pad - removal and refitting

1   Remove the instrument cluster and the centre switch panel, as described in Chapter 9.
2   Remove the steering column shroud, unbolt the upper bracket nuts and lower the column away from the fascia panel.
3   Extract the plastic clips from the lower edge of the crash pad, then peel the pad upwards and disengage its upper turned-over edge from its anchorage (Fig. 11.22).
4   Refit by reversing the removal operations, but use new plastic clips as the originals will be deformed during extraction.

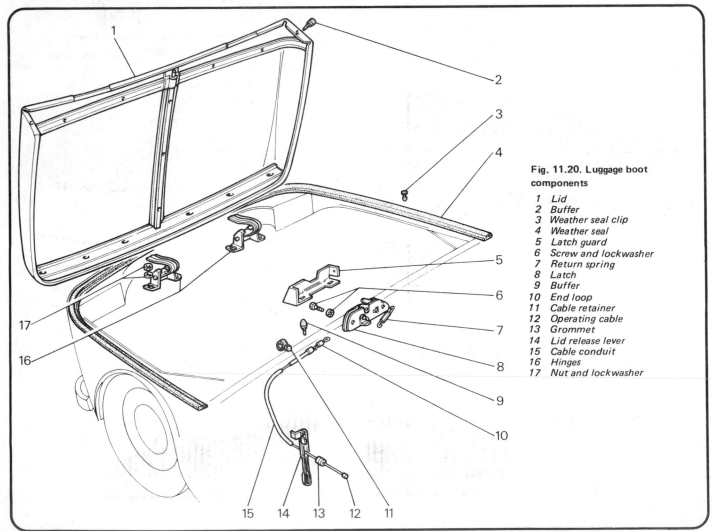

Fig. 11.20. Luggage boot components

1   Lid
2   Buffer
3   Weather seal clip
4   Weather seal
5   Latch guard
6   Screw and lockwasher
7   Return spring
8   Latch
9   Buffer
10 End loop
11 Cable retainer
12 Operating cable
13 Grommet
14 Lid release lever
15 Cable conduit
16 Hinges
17 Nut and lockwasher

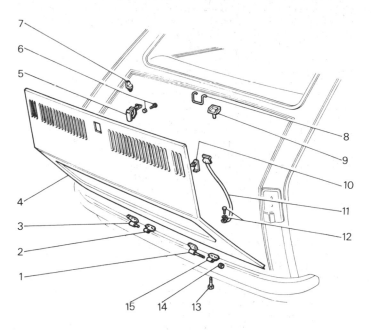

Fig. 11.21. Engine compartment lid components

1	Hinge with locknut	9	Buffer
2	Hinge plate	10	Check strap upper retainer
3	Hinge without nut	11	Check strap
4	Lid	12	Securing screw and washers
5	Latch	13	Hinge screw
6	Screw and washer	14	Self-locking nut
7	Buffer	15	Hinge plate
8	Striker		

Fig. 11.22. Instrument panel crash pad securing fasteners

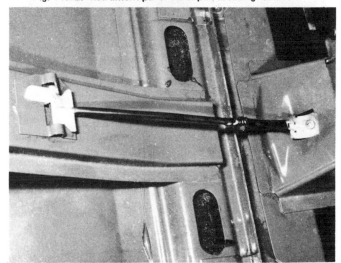

19.2 Engine compartment lid check strap

21 Sunroof - removal and installation

1 Removal of the sunroof for repair or renewal of the fabric is quite straight forward provided the means of access to the securing nuts and screws is understood.

2 Fold back the hood and using a screwdriver, prise the covers from the pivot nuts at the lower end of each side strut (Fig. 11.23).

3 Unscrew and remove the row of screws from the lower rear edge of the roof opening (Fig. 11.24).

4 Extract the two screws which are located one at each end of the rear anchor strip (Fig. 11.25).

5 Installation is a reversal of removal, but note that the pins which secure the covers on the strut nuts are pushed into place **after** the covers have been refitted.

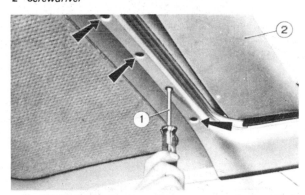

Fig. 11.23. Removing sun roof strut nut cover

1	Cover	3	Cover retaining pin
2	Screwdriver		

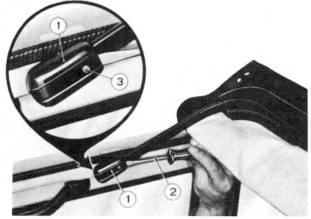

Fig. 11.24. Extracting screw from rear edge of sun roof

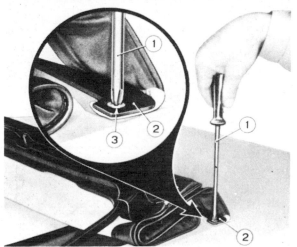

Fig. 11.25. Extracting screw from sun roof rear anchor strip

22 Air inlet and outlet grilles - removal and refitting

1   The engine air cooling inlet grilles can be removed from the rear sides of the body by first extracting the two retaining screws.
2   Using two screwdrivers as levers, prise the grille from its location. Reasonable leverage will be required for this as the resistance of the lips of the weatherseal must be overcome (Fig. 11.26).
3   The air inlet scoops can be removed from the upper corners of the engine compartment simply by extracting the securing screws.
4   The stale air outlets from the car interior are located on each (door closure) body pillar edge. To remove the grille, prise out the lower securing pin with a screwdriver and then pull the grille outwards and downwards to disengage its tag at the top edge from the bodywork (Fig. 11.27).
5   Refitting in all cases is a reversal of removal.

Fig. 11.26. Engine cooling air inlet grille removal

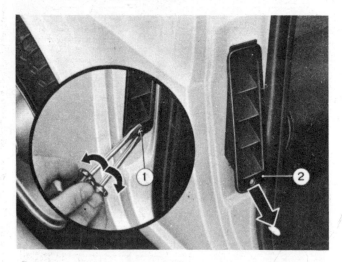

Fig. 11.27. Car interior air outlet

    1   Lower retainer   *2   Grille*

23 Exhaust gas safety baffle

1   In order to obviate the possibility of exhaust gas being drawn back into the interior of the bodyframe box sections and subsequently entering the car interior, baffle plates are located below the rear body panel as shown (Fig. 11.28).
2   Keep the securing screws tight and renew the plates at once if they become perforated due to corrosion.

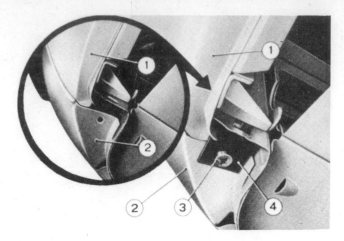

Fig. 11.28. Exhaust gas safety baffle

1 Rear body panel	*3*	*Baffle securing screw*
2 Body side panel	*4*	*Baffle*

24 Bumpers - removal and refitting

1   The front bumper mounting nuts are accessible from within the luggage boot.
2   Unscrew the nuts and withdraw the bumper bar complete with bolts, tubular spacers and brackets (Fig. 11.29).
3   Removal of the rear bumper is similar, the nuts being accessible on the inside of the body rear panel. Before removing the bumper however, disconnect the electrical connector on the lead to the rear number plate lamp (Fig. 11.30).

25 Rear seat - removal and refitting

1   To remove the rear seat cushion, grip the front edge of the seat and lift it sharply upwards to disengage it from its securing dowels (Fig. 11.31).
2   Pull the seat forward and remove it from the car.
3   To remove the seat backrest, bend down the securing tags at the base of the upholstery trim and then push the backrest upwards to disengage the locating tongues from the loops on the backrest.
4   Refitting is a reversal of removal (Fig. 11.32).

26 Interior grab handle - removal and refitting

1   The grab handle is secured by two self-tapping screws. Removal of the screw covers can sometimes prove baffling and they are in fact simply slid off the ends of the handle.
2   If they seem rather tight, persuade them gently by inserting a screwdriver blade at their open ends from which the grab handle emerges (Fig. 11.33).

27 Rear interior trim panels - removal and refitting

1   The trim panel is secured by plastic clips.
2   The clips should be withdrawn using a suitable blade to lever them out (Fig. 11.34).
3   The panel can then be lifted away.
4   A supply of new plastic clips should be on hand as the originals are usually deformed or destroyed during removal.

28 Interior rear view mirror

1   The interior rear view mirror is integral with the interior lamp and the securing screws for the complete unit are accessible after removing the lamp lens. The screws engage in tapped holes in the bodywork.

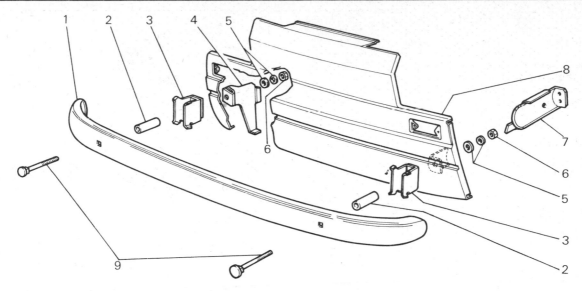

Fig. 11.29. Front bumper components

1	Bumper bar	4	Plate	6	Nuts	8	Front body panel
2	Spacer tubes	5	Washers	7	Plate	9	Mounting bolts
3	Brackets						

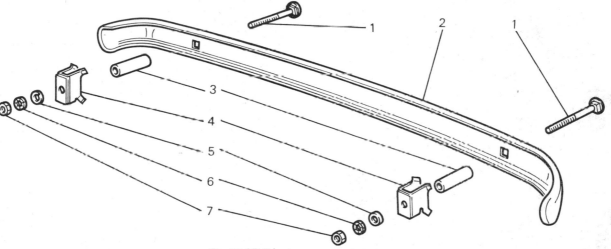

Fig. 11.30. Rear bumper components

1	Mounting bolts	3	Spacer tubes	5	Washers	7	Nuts
2	Bumper bar	4	Brackets	6	Lockwashers		

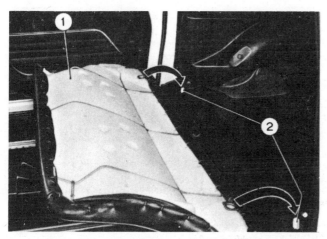

Fig. 11.31. Rear seat cushion removal

1	Cushion inverted	2	Positioning dowels

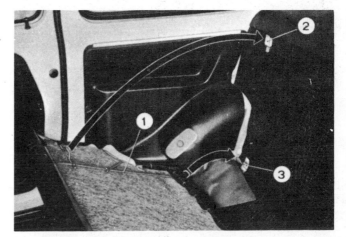

Fig. 11.32. Rear seat back removed

1	Seat back	3	Lower securing tabs
2	Tongues for securing loops		

Fig. 11.33. Grab handle detail

1 Securing screw cover
2 Grab handle
3 Securing screw

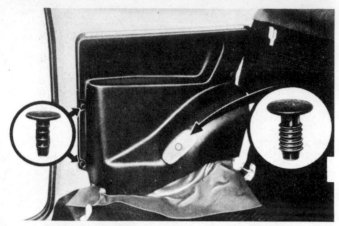

Fig. 11.34. Rear interior panel and fasteners

Fig. 11.35. Interior lamp/mirror assembly

1 Screw holes   2 Lamp lead connectors

Metric conversion tables

Inches	Decimals	Millimetres	Millimetres to Inches		Inches to Millimetres	
			mm	Inches	Inches	mm
1/64	0.015625	0.3969	0.01	0.00039	0.001	0.0254
1/32	0.03125	0.7937	0.02	0.00079	0.002	0.0508
3/64	0.046875	1.1906	0.03	0.00118	0.003	0.0762
1/16	0.0625	1.5875	0.04	0.00157	0.004	0.1016
5/64	0.078125	1.9844	0.05	0.00197	0.005	0.1270
3/32	0.09375	2.3812	0.06	0.00236	0.006	0.1524
7/64	0.109375	2.7781	0.07	0.00276	0.007	0.1778
1/8	0.125	3.1750	0.08	0.00315	0.008	0.2032
9/64	0.140625	3.5719	0.09	0.00354	0.009	0.2286
5/32	0.15625	3.9687	0.1	0.00394	0.01	0.254
11/64	0.171875	4.3656	0.2	0.00787	0.02	0.508
3/16	0.1875	4.7625	0.3	0.1181	0.03	0.762
13/64	0.203125	5.1594	0.4	0.01575	0.04	1.016
7/32	0.21875	5.5562	0.5	0.01969	0.05	1.270
15/64	0.234275	5.9531	0.6	0.02362	0.06	1.524
1/4	0.25	6.3500	0.7	0.02756	0.07	1.778
17/64	0.265625	6.7469	0.8	0.3150	0.08	2.032
9/32	0.28125	7.1437	0.9	0.03543	0.09	2.286
19/64	0.296875	7.5406	1	0.03937	0.1	2.54
5/16	0.3125	7.9375	2	0.07874	0.2	5.08
21/64	0.328125	8.3344	3	0.11811	0.3	7.62
11/32	0.34375	8.7312	4	0.15748	0.4	10.16
23/64	0.359375	9.1281	5	0.19685	0.5	12.70
3/8	0.375	9.5250	6	0.23622	0.6	15.24
25/64	0.390625	9.9219	7	0.27559	0.7	17.78
13/32	0.40625	10.3187	8	0.31496	0.8	20.32
27/64	0.421875	10.7156	9	0.35433	0.9	22.86
7/16	0.4375	11.1125	10	0.39270	1	25.4
29/64	0.453125	11.5094	11	0.43307	2	50.8
15/32	0.46875	11.9062	12	0.47244	3	76.2
31/64	0.484375	12.3031	13	0.51181	4	101.6
1/2	0.5	12.7000	14	0.55118	5	127.0
33/64	0.515625	13.0969	15	0.59055	6	152.4
17/32	0.53125	13.4937	16	0.62992	7	177.8
35/64	0.546875	13.8906	17	0.66929	8	203.2
9/16	0.5625	14.2875	18	0.70866	9	228.6
37/64	0.578125	14.6844	19	0.74803	10	254.0
19/32	0.59375	15.0812	20	0.78740	11	279.4
39/64	0.609375	15.4781	21	0.82677	12	304.8
5/8	0.625	15.8750	22	0.86614	13	330.2
41/64	0.640625	16.2719	23	0.90551	14	355.6
21/32	0.65625	16.6687	24	0.94488	15	381.0
43/64	0.671875	17.0656	25	0.98425	16	406.4
11/16	0.6875	17.4625	26	1.02362	17	431.8
45/64	0.703125	17.8594	27	1.06299	18	457.2
23/32	0.71875	18.2562	28	1.10236	19	482.6
47/64	0.734375	18.6531	29	1.14173	20	508.0
3/4	0.75	19.0500	30	1.18110	21	533.4
49/64	0.765625	19.4469	31	1.22047	22	558.8
25/32	0.78125	19.8437	32	1.25984	23	584.2
51/64	0.796875	20.2406	33	1.29921	24	609.6
13/16	0.8125	20.6375	34	1.33858	25	635.0
53/64	0.828125	21.0344	35	1.37795	26	660.4
27/32	0.84375	21.4312	36	1.41732	27	685.8
55/64	0.859375	21.8281	37	1.4567	28	711.2
7/8	0.875	22.2250	38	1.4961	29	736.6
57/64	0.890625	22.6219	39	1.5354	30	762.0
29/32	0.90625	23.0187	40	1.5748	31	787.4
59/64	0.921875	23.4156	41	1.6142	32	812.8
15/16	0.9375	23.8125	42	1.6535	33	838.2
61/64	0.953125	24.2094	43	1.6929	34	863.6
31/32	0.96875	24.6062	44	1.7323	35	889.0
63/64	0.984375	25.0031	45	1.7717	36	914.4

1   Imperial gallon = 8 Imp pints = 1.16 US gallons = 277.42 cu in = 4.5459 litres

1   US gallon = 4 US quarts = 0.862 Imp gallon = 231 cu in = 3.785 litres

1   Litre = 0.2199 Imp gallon = 0.2642 US gallon = 61.0253 cu in = 1000 cc

Miles to Kilometres		Kilometres to Miles	
1	1.61	1	0.62
2	3.22	2	1.24
3	4.83	3	1.86
4	6.44	4	2.49
5	8.05	5	3.11
6	9.66	6	3.73
7	11.27	7	4.35
8	12.88	8	4.97
9	14.48	9	5.59
10	16.09	10	6.21
20	32.19	20	12.43
30	48.28	30	18.64
40	64.37	40	24.85
50	80.47	50	31.07
60	96.56	60	37.28
70	112.65	70	43.50
80	128.75	80	49.71
90	144.84	90	55.92
100	160.93	100	62.14

lb f ft to Kg f m		Kg f m to lb f ft		$lb\ f/in^2 : Kg\ f/cm^2$		$Kg\ f/cm^2 : lb\ f/in^2$	
1	0.138	1	7.233	1	0.07	1	14.22
2	0.276	2	14.466	2	0.14	2	28.50
3	0.414	3	21.699	3	0.21	3	42.67
4	0.553	4	28.932	4	0.28	4	56.89
5	0.691	5	36.165	5	0.35	5	71.12
6	0.829	6	43.398	6	0.42	6	85.34
7	0.967	7	50.631	7	0.49	7	99.56
8	1.106	8	57.864	8	0.56	8	113.79
9	1.244	9	65.097	9	0.63	9	128.00
10	1.382	10	62.330	10	0.70	10	142.23
20	2.765	20	144.660	20	1.41	20	284.47
30	4.147	30	216.990	30	2.11	30	426.70

Index